AFRICA*trek*

AFRIC

A *trek*

A JOURNEY BY BICYCLE THROUGH AFRICA

Written and photographed by
DAN BUETTNER

LERNER PUBLICATIONS COMPANY/MINNEAPOLIS

Additional photographs courtesy of: p. 22 (middle), Anadarko
Petroleum Corporation; p. 37, © Irma Turtle; p. 44 (bottom),
Carol Barker; p. 73 (top left), John Vreyens; p. 73 (top right),
Daniel H. Condit. All maps by Laura Westlund. Recipe on page 81
adapted from Hultman, Tami, ed. *Africa News Cookbook*. Durham:
Africa News Service, 1985.

Words in **bold type** are listed in a glossary that begins on
page 109.

LIBRARY OF CONGRESS CATALOGING-IN-PUBLICATION DATA

Buettner, Dan
  Africatrek: a journey by bicycle through Africa / written and
photographed by Dan Buettner.
      p. cm.
  Includes index.
  ISBN 0-8225-2951-3 (lib. bdg.: alk. paper)
  1. Buettner, Dan—Africa—Journeys—Juvenile literature.
2. Africa—Description and travel—Juvenile literature. 3. Africa—
Description and travel. I. Title.
DT12.25.B84   1996
916.04'329—dc20   96-3954

Manufactured in the United States of America
1 2 3 4 5 6 - JR - 02 01 00 99 98 97

CONTENTS

For my two beloved Irenes—
one for her wisdom,
the other for her promise

A NOTE FROM THE AUTHOR

"Life is a risky adventure, or it is nothing."

Helen Keller, who was blind and deaf most of her life, wrote those words when she was 77 years old. She may have lived in darkness and silence, but Helen Keller clearly understood how an explorer thinks. It doesn't matter if the explorer climbs the highest mountains, dogsleds to the North Pole, or, in my case, bicycles across continents.

My life as an explorer began in 1986 when three friends and I bicycled from Alaska to

Argentina. We set a Guinness Book world record, but since that journey, I've come to value the experience more than the record. I learned more about the world—and my place in it—during 305 days on my bicycle than I'd learned in 16 years of school. I also discovered the addictive excitement of waking every morning and having the road unfold before you.

In 1990 my brother Steve and I teamed up with two Russians to bicycle around the world by way of the former Soviet Union. During that trek, Sovietrek as we called it, I learned that there is power in diversity and that the best team is one whose members come from a variety of racial, cultural, and educational backgrounds.

Dan Buettner's brother Steve *(left)* has been part of every trek. Here he pushes his bike through the highlands of Cameroon in central Africa.

So when my brother and I picked Dr. Chip Thomas as our first teammate for Africatrek—our continental crossing of Africa—one of the reasons was because he was an African American. Chip also brought to the team the skills of a physician and the experience of being a minority in a world that doesn't always treat minorities fairly. Steve and I could learn from him, particularly because in Africa we would be the minority.

I first saw a picture of Chip in a mail-order catalog. He was wearing colorful clothing and long **dreadlocks** and was taking the blood pressure of one of his Navajo patients. When I called him at his home in Kaibeto, Arizona, he told me that he was off to New Zealand to enjoy a three-month bike ride that he'd won in a photo contest.

"How would you like a free, 10-month bike trip in Africa?" I said. There was a long silence.

"I'll call you back," he replied.

It took him three months to finally accept the challenge of the trek.

Finding two African cyclists, for separate parts of the trip, would make our team complete. After sifting through 54 candidates, we chose a Nigerian cyclist named Mobolaji Oduyoye (or "Bo," as we called him) and Mike Mpyangu of Uganda.

Bo was a tall, soft-spoken man who had been educated in France and spoke three African languages. We chose him for his patience, his understanding of African formalities, and his spiritual strength. He'd pedal with us on the first leg from Tunisia to Uganda. There we'd pick up Mike, and Bo would return to Nigeria.

Steve and I first heard about Mike in 1991 on a day when we got three faxes—one from Boston, another from New York, and a third from El Salvador.

With Steve looking on, Chip Thomas *(above)* showed a young Tunisian boy a snapshot of the boy and his friends. The bikes that Dan *(below)* and the team rode carried large containers of water.

They all recommended Mike, an experienced guide and a disciplined, thoughtful person. He'd accompany Steve and me from Uganda to South Africa, the end-point of Africatrek.

All team members agreed on two goals—we'd show the world that black people and white people could co-operate even under the most difficult conditions and we'd set a Guinness Book world record for crossing Africa.

Each of us rode a 24-speed Cannondale mountain bike full of equipment. Steve, the youngest member of the team, had a typical load. His bike was weighed down with a sleeping bag, half of a tent, a water purifier, books, clothes, and just about everything you'd need for a 10-month bike ride. But Steve was also our mechanic and camera operator. This meant he carried most of the heavy bike tools and replacement parts, as well as a miniature television camera.

On Chip's bike, in addition to the usual stuff, was a variety of medicine—everything from needles to malaria pills. Bo brought dictionaries and translation books. Into my bags, I stowed the satellite equipment that would help us cross the Sahara.

The Africatrek team also included Mobolaji (Bo) Oduyoye *(above)* from Nigeria and Mike Mpyangu *(right)* from Uganda.

Perhaps the greatest challenge of organizing a ride like Africatrek is raising the money. In addition to trip expenses, we were committed to making the journey an educational opportunity for school kids. With the help of a Minnesota university, we developed and printed 50,000 study guides. (We'd also be hooked up to the Internet.) Between the trek and the guides, the

The team wore T-shirts marked with the Africatrek logo, or emblem *(top)*. Each bike was loaded with a variety of supplies *(above)*, including a repair kit, clothing, a sleeping bag, and part of a tent.

price tag came to $230,000!

We started contacting big corporations for help. For every hundred or so tries, we'd get one corporation to come aboard. It took 14 months and several thousand letters before we had enough sponsors to pay the bills. The only things left were to decide on a route and to get official documents.

We knew we wanted to bike from the top of Africa to the bottom—a distance of about 12,000 miles. The route, we discovered, is best not planned too rigidly.

Every country requires a visitor to have an entry document called a visa. Visas almost always come with a time limit, forcing you to predict when you're going to arrive and leave a country. This is difficult to do when you're on a bike. Political troubles, shortages of water, and sudden outbreaks of disease can force the traveler to change the route at any moment. So we didn't

Panniers, or storage bags that hang from bikes, helped the team haul their equipment *(top)*, some of which was unpacked when they made camp *(above)*.

get visas ahead of time. We listened nightly to the BBC World Service on our pocket shortwave radio and visited the U.S. Embassy in every capital city for information. This approach made Africatrek an ever-unfolding mystery.

INTRODUCTION

Traveling in Africa is a risky adventure no matter how you go. It's the second largest continent on earth, with the biggest desert, the tallest freestanding mountain, and the second largest tropical rain forest. Diseases like malaria, leprosy, AIDS, Ebola, and diarrhea kill millions of people every year. Wars and starvation take the lives of millions more.

But that's the bad news. Newspapers often overlook the good news. For example, Africa has huge reserves of gold and diamonds. It has more than 1,000 sepa-rate cultures and languages.

It's also a continent of opposites. The vast emptiness of the Sahara Desert contrasts with crowds of Nigeria. Fertile land exists in countries that can't feed their people. Snow covers Mount Kilimanjaro in Tanzania above the steamy heat of the tropics. Brutal wars exist alongside kindhearted people.

In Zaire a woman with a broken bicycle carried it home on her head.

Although we studied a lot about Africa before we left, the real story unfolded day by day. Our journey took us through 14 of Africa's 52 countries. In **North Africa,** we sniffed the cool breezes of the Mediterranean Sea and sped through the rugged Atlas Mountains of Tunisia and Algeria. By pedaling southward, we entered the huge Sahara Desert to reach Niger and then Nigeria, the largest country in **West Africa.**

From a cool and dry climate, we biked for weeks through hot, wet, humid weather in Cameroon, the Central African Republic, and Zaire. By the time we ended up in **East Africa**—the location of Uganda, Kenya, Tanzania, and Malawi—the climate had become a little easier to handle. Our journey in **southern Africa** took us through war-torn Mozambique and spectacular Zimbabwe to our final destination at Cape Agulhas, South Africa.

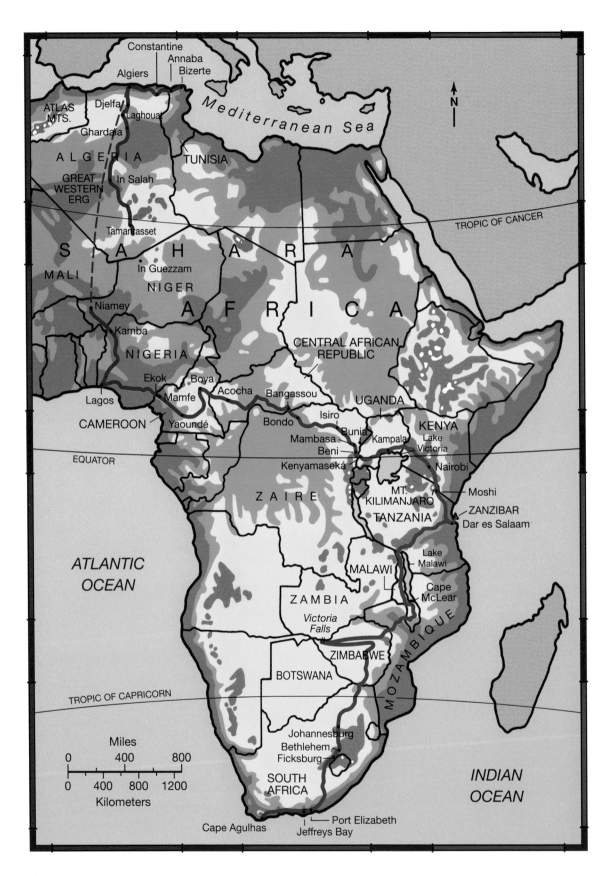

Constantine
Annaba
Bizerte
Algiers
Djelfa
ATLAS
MTS.
Ghardaïa
Laghouat

Mediterranean Sea

N

ALGERIA
TUNISIA
GREAT
WESTERN
ERG
In Salah

TROPIC OF CANCER

Tamanrasset

S A H A R A

MALI
In Guezzam
NIGER
A F R I C A

Niamey
Kamba
NIGERIA
CENTRAL AFRICAN
REPUBLIC
Ekok   Boya
Mamfe   Acocha
Lagos   Bangassou
UGANDA
CAMEROON   Yaoundé
Bondo   Isiro   KENYA
Mambasa   Bunia   Lake
Beni   Kampala   Victoria
EQUATOR
Kenyamasekā   Nairobi
MT.   Moshi
KILIMANJARO
Z A I R E   ZANZIBAR
TANZANIA   Dar es Salaam

ATLANTIC
OCEAN

Lake
Malawi
MALAWI
Cape
McLear
ZAMBIA
*Victoria
Falls*
ZIMBABWE
BOTSWANA
MOZAMBIQUE

TROPIC OF CAPRICORN

Miles
0   400   800

0   400   800   1200
Kilometers

Johannesburg
Bethlehem
Ficksburg

SOUTH
AFRICA
INDIAN
OCEAN

Cape Agulhas   Port Elizabeth
Jeffreys Bay

Throughout these varied scenes, we heard many languages, including Arabic, Swahili, French, and English, as well as local dialects. We encountered the many religions of Africa, too. **Islam,** founded in the Middle East, dominates much of North and West Africa. Christian missionaries have had an impact on parts of central, eastern, and southern Africa, but Islam also has a strong presence there. In some places, people continue to follow traditions that predate any of the

The average life expectancy for a person born on the African continent is 55.

world's large, organized religions.

It took us 262 days to cycle through Africa. On a good day, we traveled 150 miles. On bad days, when there was sand or mud or no road at all, we were lucky to log 20 miles.

I believe the bicycle is the ideal means of transportation, because it forces you to go slow, to observe your surroundings, and to meet people. At 12 miles per hour—our average speed during Africa-trek—we not only had the opportunity to see more but also to hear things, feel things, and even smell things. The

sound of children singing, a cooling breeze, the smell of roasting meat all became part of our travel experience.

Bicycles gave us the chance to see what it's really like to live in Africa, a continent with the reputation for war, disease, and poverty. But Africa will fool you.

It's true that about one of three African children doesn't get enough to eat. But then again, African children don't eat junk food, fats, and preservatives like American kids do. What's worse: too much or too little? I'm not sure.

Eighteen of the world's twenty poorest countries are in Africa. That's a horrible statistic. But how do you measure poverty? Because people don't have money, does that mean they're poor? Does happiness mean having lots of things? I'm not sure, but because of Africa-trek I learned to look at these questions and indeed our world in a very different way.

The team stopped at a school in Cameroon where the children were just finishing their morning prayers.

EIGHT WHEELS SOUTHWARD

Only 11,999 miles left to go!" Steve shouted back to us after we had pedaled the first mile of our journey through Africa. It was November 29, 1992, and we were in Bizerte, Tunisia. Steve, Chip, Bo, and I had just dipped our rear wheels in the Mediterranean Sea.

We began pedaling through mazelike streets lined with whitewashed buildings, colorful markets, and mosques (Islamic houses of prayer). It was a warm, sunny morning, and the four of us were excited to begin our adventure.

Outside Bizerte, we turned west and followed the fantastically rugged northern coast toward Algeria. Northern Africa, or the **Maghrib,** didn't look like the Africa I'd imagined.

From Bizerte, Tunisia, after dipping the wheels of their bikes in the Mediterranean Sea, the team headed westward. At one restaurant along the way, a cow's head *(inset)* hung outside as an advertisement for lunch.

Instead of rain forests, pine and eucalyptus trees covered the hills that rolled away from our road. No lions or elephants roam this far north. Instead burros pulled ancient plows though olive groves, and children herded goats. Occasionally we'd see a cow's head dangling outside a restaurant to attract motorists for lunch. Black people like Chip and Bo were rare, and they often drew long stares from the mainly Islamic population.

Trouble began on the second day. Chip, the oldest team member, was lagging behind. His knees and behind hurt. His usual good nature had turned sour.

"This is a bad sign," Steve whispered to me. "We're only doing 60 miles a day and Chip already looks like he's going to die. You know we have to start covering a hundred miles a day pretty soon if we're going to set the record. What's going to happen then?"

Near the Tunisian border with Algeria, as Chip struggled up a hill, a man leaned out of his car and screamed, "Get out of our country!" I figured the guy was mad because Chip was in the road, but to Chip the message meant something else—as a black man, he was not welcome in this part of Africa.

At the border, Bo got some crushing news. The Algerian government would not issue him a visa. I guessed it was because Algeria and Nigeria were having political disagreements. Chip saw it as another act of racism.

Regardless, it meant that Bo would have to turn back and meet us on the other side of Algeria.

The detour would cost time and money. In

SOLDIERS WITH MACHINE GUNS RIFLED THROUGH OUR PACKS.

addition, Algeria itself was a problem. The ninth biggest country on earth, Algeria is dominated by the Sahara Desert. We had no idea how long it would take

us to cross the country or where we'd end up. Where and when were we supposed to meet Bo on the other side? We shook his hand and told him that we would leave a message with his parents in Nigeria when we knew where we'd be. But we silently feared that we'd never see him again.

At the Algerian border, outside the city of Annaba, soldiers with machine guns rifled though our packs, dumping everything on the floor. They suspected us of carrying drugs. One soldier, wearing sunglasses and speaking French, waved

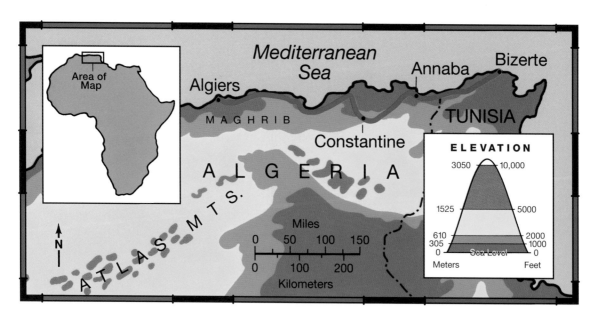

(Below) **In western Tunisia, Bo, Chip, and Steve posed with some of the locals. Soon afterward Bo was denied entry into Algeria. He rejoined the team after they reached Niger.** (Left) **Team members ate PowerBars to keep up their energy, but guards near Annaba, Algeria, wrongly thought the bars were drugs.**

Chip to the side of the road. Steve and I followed. He dug through Chip's pack and pulled out a chocolate-flavored PowerBar.

"Drugs?" he charged.

"No," I replied in French. "It's food made especially for athletes." I had to rip off a wrapper to prove it to him.

Steve biked through a tunnel outside Constantine, a fortified city that lies more than 800 feet above a river valley in Algeria.

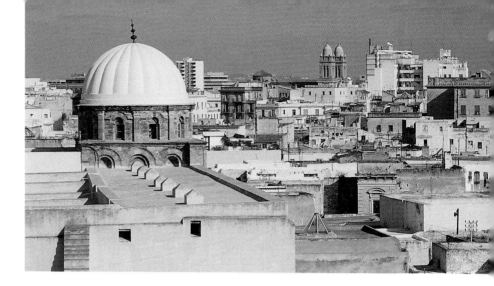

The team eventually reached Algiers, the Algerian capital. The city features whitewashed architecture *(right and below)* and well-stocked markets *(bottom)*.

After leaving Annaba, we arrived in Algiers, a Mediterranean port with a crumbling Casbah (fortress) and sprawling high-rises. It's also the capital of Algeria with urban problems like most big cities around the world. Litter flowed down the streets, and antigovernment graffiti covered buildings. My

introduction to the city was witnessing a young Algerian firing on the government building with a pistol. Police beat him to the ground and dragged him away.

We nonetheless had a pleasant four-day stay. Our $4-per-night hotel room got us cold showers, a sagging bed, and a breakfast of strong, sweet coffee and French bread with jam and butter. Steve overhauled the bikes, while Chip and I taped news segments that we sent back to the United States for the first of several television reports. At night we walked to downtown restaurants, where we could get an excellent meal for under $3.00. We then rushed back to our hotel before the 10:00 P.M. curfew. People caught on the streets after that hour might be shot.

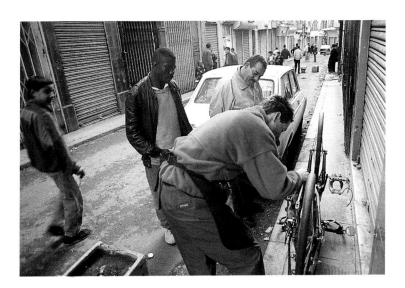

After only a few weeks, the bikes were already in need of Steve's mechanical skills.

TEA AND COOKIES

Chip and I love to take pictures, especially of people. We once saw three shepherd girls standing outside their simple desert home. Chip and I pulled out our cameras but managed to terrify the oldest girl, who scurried into the house.

We were afraid she'd gone to tell her father. But when she returned a few minutes later she presented us with tea and cookies on a silver platter!

TEA
IN THE
SAHARA

From Algiers Steve, Chip, and I pedaled our bikes for a day up 4,200 feet over the Atlas Mountains. The road switched back and forth through cool, misty pine forests. Near a pass, the trees began to thin as grazing land and vineyards replaced them. When we coasted down the other side of the pass, the fields gave way to dry pastures. We saw people called Chaamba Arabs tending herds of skinny goats and sheep.

By nightfall we saw only prickly bushes growing out of the arid, sandy land. The road shot out from underneath our tires like a giant strip of black electrical tape and disappeared at a point on the horizon. After several hours of seeing no trees, no animals, and no buildings, we pulled our bikes to the side of the road. To the west, the giant orange disk of the sun sank beyond the horizon. It left behind a rosy haze and the feeling of great emptiness. We were standing in the doorway of the Sahara Desert— the beginning of the **trans-Saharan Highway.**

Chip and Steve cycled the trans-Saharan Highway, a modern road that traces an ancient trade route for camel caravans.

The Sahara has been described as an enormous beach in search of an ocean. Huge sand dunes called **ergs** cover a fifth of it. But there are also flattopped hills, high plateaus, and towering, treeless mountains. **Wadis** (dry riverbeds) create a web in parts of the desert that looks like the veins in your forearm. In many places, the wadis fill with water only once every few years when the rain comes.

The most common landscape, though, is the **Tanezrouft,** a vast plateau stretching for hundreds of miles. A person can bike there for days and see nothing bigger than a rock the size of a baseball.

The trans-Saharan Highway took us through the towns of Djelfa and Laghouat to the big **oasis** of Ghardaïa. Not only did the landscape of southern Algeria change from that of the north, but the people did, too. They got nicer.

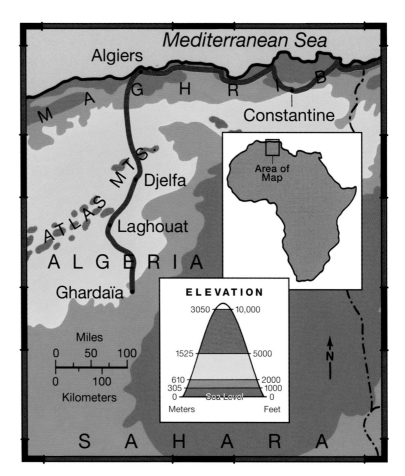

Algerian kids played soccer amid the shifting sand dunes of the Great Western Erg.

The team stopped in the desert to take their midday meal.

Ghardaïa is an oasis (fertile area) about 300 miles south of Algiers. Although located in the Sahara, the oasis supports a population of many thousands of people.

Here's an example. Chip, Steve, and I were sitting in the sand on the side of the road eating a skimpy lunch of dates and powdered milk. A truck slowed, and a man stood up in the back, threw us a bunch of fresh carrots, and waved. While Steve was picking up the carrots, a car traveling from the other direction stopped. Another traveler got out and handed him an armful of tangerines and a baguette. *"Bon chance!"* he hollered, wishing us good luck as he drove away.

Five days of hard biking took us to Ghardaïa, where we arrived in mid-December of 1992. We saw the tops of the palm trees first. They stuck out like lettuce greens from a salad bowl. As we neared, a wadi surrounded by five separate settlements appeared. They, too, seemed to pop out of the nearby hills as if they had risen out of the sand.

Colorful rugs lined a narrow market street in Ghardaïa.

The people who live in Ghardaïa—the Mzabites—survive because of water. Although it rains only once or twice a year and Ghardaïa looked bone dry, the oasis was dotted with roughly 200,000 date palm trees, and homes on the town's outskirts had green gardens.

It was dark when the three of us rolled into town. We walked our bikes through streets so narrow we could touch walls on either side

Dan captured the shy look of a young Algerian girl.

While looking at the sights, we also searched for a place to stay. But all of the hotels were full. In addition, no one was willing to let us camp on their property. We were facing a cold night in the desert when we heard a voice from behind us say good evening.

Dates are a desert mainstay and grow in bunches on palm trees.

with outstretched arms. Unlike towns in northern Algeria, not a candy wrapper littered the streets, nor did a pencil mark mar the buildings. The shops werc clean, bright, and well stocked.

The men were dressed in white skull-caps and billowy pants that narrowed at the ankle. The women wore veils that covered them from head to toe, a choice that we learned was an Islamic gesture of modesty.

Most Algerians follow the Islamic religion, which en-courages women to wear full-length coverings as a sign of modesty.

29

We turned to see a teenager wearing a *djellaba* (a loose garment with a hood). Only his curly black hair, his face, and his smile showed from under the headgear.

"Where do you come from?" he asked in French.

"America," I replied.

"America!" he repeated. "I've never met a real American. I'm very glad to meet you."

He introduced himself as Abdul and asked, "Where are you going at this late hour?"

We told him our problem with finding a place to sleep.

"You mustn't stay in the desert at night," Abdul warned. "It's dangerous. You could step on a sand viper."

He led us through Ghardaïa's streets to his family's home on the edge of town. Inside a sandstone and mortar house, he showed us three beds and bid us good night.

We awoke the next morning to the sound of metal clinking on glass. I walked outside, where I saw that Abdul had laid out a carpet under a palm tree. He was pouring sweet mint tea in glass cups and had set out small metal plates of pomegranates, dates, and oranges—all grown in his family's garden.

"Good day, my friends!" he said in greeting. "Come. Have breakfast."

As we ate, Abdul explained that the ancestors of his people had come to the oasis 900 years ago and had lived as traders. Many of the townspeople had grown rich. Inside their 500-

Abdul, a young resident of Ghardaïa, helped the team find shelter and later explained how dates can thrive in a desert climate.

Chip enjoyed tea and a breakfast of fruit grown in Abdul's garden.

year-old homes, they had TVs, VCRs, and satellite dishes.

"Why do older women wear those head-to-toe veils?" I asked.

"It's not only older women," he replied. "As soon as a girl turns 12 she starts to wear a veil. For the rest of her life, only the males in her family will see her face."

"Would you make your wife wear one?"

"Of course, but she also would want to. It's tradition, and it makes women free—free from having to dress up and look pretty, free from getting hassled by strange men."

We took a walk in the garden. Abdul showed me the fruit trees that had produced our breakfast and neat rows of carrots, onions, and tomatoes. I asked him how all this could grow in the middle of the Sahara.

Abdul explained that the fruit trees—especially the date trees—have very long roots that reach deeply into underground streams to get the water they need to grow. In addition, behind the garden, a rocky slope led to a fairly large holding tank. Although the tank filled up with rainwater only once or twice a year, it

kept Abdul's garden well watered.

I told him that in the United States we watered our gardens with sprinklers and further helped them grow with chemicals called fertilizers. He looked puzzled. Then I asked him what he thought of America.

"We think most American people are good," he said. "I think American girls with blond hair and blue eyes are beautiful."

"Could you marry an American?" I asked.

"Never," he replied abruptly. "If I married an American girl, who would marry the Mzabite girl?"

A RISKY ADVENTURE

Things got tough when we left Ghardaïa. A 40-mile-per-hour headwind started blowing out of the south. It picked up fistfuls of sand and hurled them into our eyes. Our daily cycling average dropped from 100 miles to less than 50. We were eating bad food and getting sick with diarrhea. We went without showers. Our skin felt like it was covered by dirty maple syrup.

Less than a month into the trek, on Thursday, December 24, temperatures climbed to more than 100°F. I'd noticed that Chip was starting to look frail. Salt from dried sweat covered his face, and his hands were chapped and peeling.

Late in the afternoon as we pedaled side by side I asked him, "Are you going to make it?"

Chip hunched over as he headed into strong winds that blew sand and grit in his face.

"I don't know," he said. "I cried this morning. I've been thinking about my grandmother who just died and how my parents will spend their first Christmas alone." He looked down and watched his feet turning the pedals. Then he lifted his head, stared straight ahead, and said, "When we hit the next oasis, I think I'm going to quit the trek and go home."

We spent Christmas Day in a place called In Salah—one of the hottest spots on earth. But because Muslims (followers of Islam) don't celebrate Christmas, it was just another Friday. Camels sauntered down the main street. Men sat in dusty cafes and drank sweet mint tea. Flies buzzed everywhere. We spent the day missing home and trying to stay cool.

We did have one piece of good luck. We met a young, French-Canadian bicyclist named Benoît Laliberté. Chip and Benoît hit it off instantly. When Benoît agreed to travel the rest of the Sahara with us, Chip's spirits lifted. He decided to keep going, at least to the next big oasis—Tamanrasset. "I'll decide then," he told Steve and me.

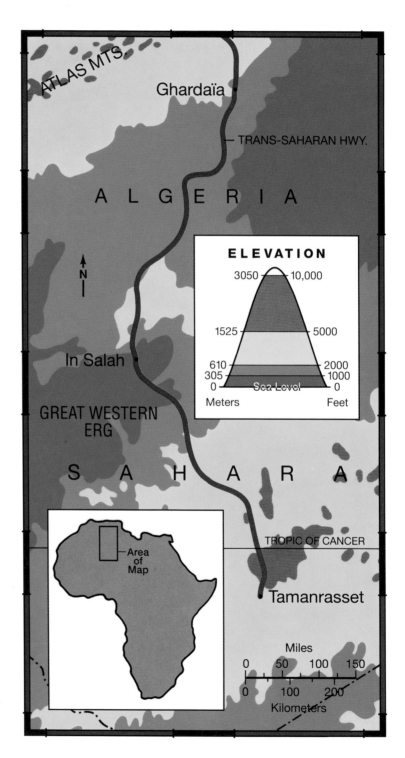

(Above) Dan, Steve, and Chip added bike treads to the other tire tracks in the Sahara. (Left) During this part of the expedition, they met Benoît Laliberté, a cyclist from Quebec, Canada. He joined, left, and rejoined the trek at various points along the route.

ground, they're hopelessly confusing. Most of the tracks lead eventually to In Guezzam, Niger, some 245 miles away. Sometimes, however, the tracks can draw travelers hundreds of miles out of the way.

This news presented a serious problem. The team could carry only five days of water on the bikes. If we took one of the wrong tracks—or if we didn't cover the 245 miles in five days—we'd run out of water. On a hot day in the Sahara without

(Above) **One of the bikes leaned against a signpost showing the distance to the oasis of Tamanrasset.** *(Below)* **The team passed the rotting carcasses of dead camels, reminding the cyclists that no living thing can survive in the desert without water.**

In Tamanrasset, four hard days later, our road ended. On a map, a red line stretched southward from Tamanrasset to Niger and the rest of Africa. This line would seem to represent a road, but the people of Tamanrasset told us a different story. They said that that "road" is really a 30-mile-wide band of tracks. From an airplane, these tracks have a clear southward direction. But, from the

water you can die in four hours.

Another concern involved the Tuareg, a nomadic desert people of the region. They were fighting with the governments of Algeria, Niger, and Mali, which have kicked the Tuareg off their traditional lands. Violence has often flared up between government soldiers and Tuareg warriors. Outsiders aren't safe from attack either.

This grim situation discouraged Chip. The second day in Tamanrasset, he again announced that he'd be leaving the trek.

Meanwhile, Steve, Benoît, and I had started making plans for crossing the open desert. First we needed a visa to enter Niger. The official at the Niger consulate charged us $30 to stamp our passport. Then he made us sign a paper saying that trying to enter Niger through the Sahara was dangerous and that we would not hold the government responsible if we were wounded or killed.

Grocery shopping was our next step. We bought dates and dried milk—the same food that camel caravans have used for centuries to cross the Sahara. We picked up five-gallon water jugs to strap to our bikes.

THE TUAREG

The Tuareg—a Berber-speaking, Muslim group—once controlled most of the trade across the Sahara. They ride camels and herd livestock. Tuareg men wear 12-foot-long purple veils wrapped around their heads. Heat and sweat cause the dye to stain their faces blue, so they are also called the Blue Men. Tuareg women also are unique. Unlike most Muslim women, they don't wear veils and hold a lot of power. For example, when a Tuareg chief dies, his sister's sons—not his own—inherit property and authority.

Mounted Tuareg travel throughout southern Algeria.

Then we tried to find an escort, someone with a vehicle. We found only one driver willing to take the job. "Very dangerous," he said. He wanted $2,000. We decided to go alone.

The day before we were to leave, we met Chip for lunch. Under a pine tree on the main street, we ate olive soup and chicken couscous. Afterward Chip opened his journal and read Helen Keller's quote, "Life is a risky adventure, or it is nothing."

He said he realized that Africatrek wasn't just a personal journey. He knew that we had made promises to sponsors, that more than a million kids were following us in their schools, and that as a doctor he was an important part of a team. He shut his journal and announced, "I'm going with you guys."

Thirty-three miles out of Tamanrasset— and about 2,000 miles into the trek—the last markings of the road ended. We began pedaling on open sand.

The trick here was to keep moving. If we stopped, our bike tires would break through the upper crust, and we'd sink. Pushing the bikes was also hard work. We could cover one, perhaps two, miles per hour.

At times we had no idea if we were traveling north, south, east, or west. We often stopped to take a GPS (Global Positioning System) reading. It uses satellites to calculate exact longitude and latitude. After finding longitude and latitude, we could navigate with a compass and a map.

Day Two on this "road" brought terrific sandstorms called **siroccos.** They blotted out the sun with a devilish brown cloud. Sand blasted our faces and arms so hard that we had to put on ski masks and rain jackets for protection. Sand crept into food, sleeping bags, and up every crevice of our bodies. We could do

nothing but stop and take shelter.

When the winds died down, we continued southward. Chip, Steve, Benoît, and I spread out like ants in a giant sandbox. Our spirits were low. Rashes, from not bathing, covered our bodies. We were tired and suffering from diarrhea. The four of us gathered around the

SAND BLASTED OUR FACES AND ARMS SO HARD THAT WE HAD TO PUT ON SKI MASKS.

fire, and Steve poured water into the pot for tea. Then he shook our plastic jug. "We're getting pretty low," he said.

For Benoît, that was the last straw. "Tomorrow I'm going back to Tamanrasset," he announced abruptly. "You guys can keep going."

"I'm with you," Chip added. Steve remained quiet.

I walked away from the fire and climbed a nearby hill. I thought about our dilemma. I knew that, as my brother and long-standing partner in adventure, Steve would do whatever I did. But I also knew that, with half the team gone, it would be more dangerous for the two of us to keep going.

I admire people who take smart risks. People who take risks, even if they don't always succeed, get a little stronger, a little smarter, or a little bolder with each try. But in the Sahara, I realized we were clearly crossing the line between risky adventure and stupidity. If I kept going, especially without Chip and Benoît, I was putting my life and my brother's life in serious danger. No adventure is worth such a risk.

The next morning sirocco winds blew out of the south creating a strong tailwind for four cyclists heading back to Tamanrasset.

THE

DETOUR

After turning around in the desert, we pedaled back to Tamanrasset. There, we met truck drivers who agreed to take us and our bikes back to Algiers. This second journey across the desert took three days and nights. After biking the desert, crossing it by truck was, as Chip commented, "like skimming a book you once studied." From Tamanrasset, we took an airplane to Niamey, the capital of Niger, to hook up with

Bo. The trip amounted to a 2,800-mile detour to avoid 200 miles of war zone.

It was late January when the Africatrek team was reunited. As we pedaled through the capital, the air was full of pulsating music and the smells of cooking fires and spices. Women carried huge trays of fruit on their heads, and street vendors sold roasted tripe (animal stomach tissue eaten as food) from flaming barrels. Kids yelled, *"Bienvenue!* (Welcome)"* as we passed.

We were south of the Sahara—an area called **sub-Saharan Africa.** Most of the Africans in this part of the continent are black people but are members of hundreds of different ethnic and language groups.

The team eventually ended up in Niamey, the capital of Niger, where they watched a weaver make straw mats and also were reunited with Bo.

Outside of Niamey, the road cut through the **Sahel,** a land covered with dry, prickly vegetation. Bicycling was not easy here. It was hot, windy, and dirty. Fine sand, blown in from the Sahara by **harmattan** winds, covered everything and blotted out the sun. It looked like an orange smudge against a milky sky. When we stopped in the first village, our bodies were coated in dust and sweat, and we were very thirsty.

Dozens of kids ran to us from their cone-shaped straw huts. Small scars on their faces, made with razors at birth, identified them as belonging to the

Using a wooden tool, a girl from the Djerma ethnic group pounded grain into flour.

Thanks to a camel and its owner, the straw goods found their way to a market in the capital.

Djerma tribe. They were barefoot and wore dirty T-shirts that said things like, "Frank's Plumbing, Tulsa" or "I'm a Toys-R-Us Kid." Most of them carried trays of food to sell.

"Can anyone find us some water?" Bo asked loudly in French. The voices fell quiet.

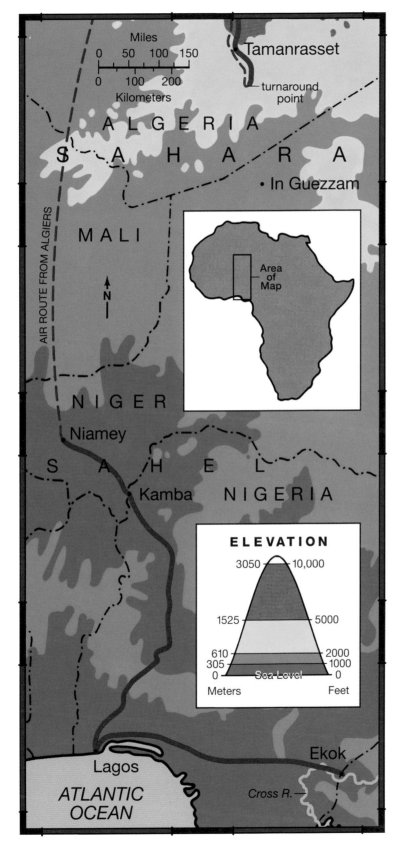

Miles
0 50 100 150
0 100 200
Kilometers

Tamanrasset

turnaround point

ALGERIA

SAHARA

• In Guezzam

AIR ROUTE FROM ALGIERS

MALI

Area of Map

N

NIGER

Niamey

SAHEL

Kamba

NIGERIA

ELEVATION

Meters		Feet
3050		10,000
1525		5000
610		2000
305		1000
0	Sea Level	0

Ekok

Lagos

ATLANTIC OCEAN

Cross R.

"Isn't there any water in this village?" Bo asked again.

After another long pause, a small boy carrying a plastic bucket pushed his way through the crowd. "This is all we have," he said meekly. Inside the bucket were four warm bottles of Coke, priced forty cents apiece.

Other kids tried to sell us food. One boy had cola nuts, which are white and the size of crab apples. They give you energy but taste like turpentine and turn your teeth red. Another kid had barbecued cow intestines, and another had a sack of things that looked like skinny dates.

"What's that?" Steve asked him.

The boy took one from the bag and held out a roasted grasshopper.

"Yuck!"

"No, sir," he replied, popping one into his mouth. "They're crunchy!"

Many insects are good for you and are an important source of protein in African diets.

Cooks in Niger, as well as in other parts of Africa, prepare insects, such as grasshoppers, to be eaten as food. Grasshoppers are reportedly quite crunchy.

We left the village and cycled for several days to reach Kamba in English-speaking Nigeria. Big and oil-rich, Nigeria is the most powerful country in West Africa. It also has a fairly bad reputation. People in Niger had talked of Nigeria as the big bully on the block. Indeed, our first look at Nigeria wasn't pleasant.

Charred fields lined the road as we cycled 622 miles from Kamba to the former Nigerian capital of Lagos. When we stopped for lunch, we found dirty, over- crowded towns where sewage ran in open gutters. Rolling wrecks sputtered down high- ways, spewing thick clouds of smoke and creating monstrous traf- fic jams that Nigerians call the "go slow."

The food took some getting used to, too. Nigerians probably eat the hottest food in Africa. We tasted a veg- etable soup that had no carrots or potatoes but contained plenty of hot peppers. Menus written on chalk boards offered things like *egusi* (a spicy melon seed soup) and pounded yam and *garri* (roots boiled and formed into gooey,

Lagos *(above)*, a sprawling urban area in Nigeria, was the capital until 1991, when Abuja replaced it.

baseball-sized lumps). There was spicy okra soup that followed the spoon to your mouth in snotlike strands.

Perhaps the most frightening food was bush meat. It would come to your table in all shapes and sizes often gristly and smothered in hot red sauce. When we asked what it was, we always got the same response: "Comes from the bush."

I learned much about Nigerians from our teammate Bo. The country has 225 tribes, each of which speaks a different language, eats different foods, and wears different clothing.

(Left) **A Nigerian vendor carried chickens to market in a manner seen throughout Africa.** (Below) **To mark the occasion of her marriage, a young woman from the Fulani ethnic group painted her hands in a ceremonial fashion.**

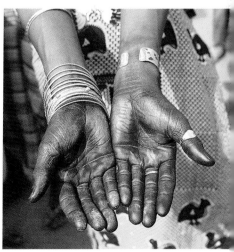

The Hausa, for example, are largely Muslim and dominate Nigeria's military. The Ibo, on the other hand, most often practice Catholicism and are known as shrewd businesspeople. Bo was Yoruba, and by his description his people are peaceful and tend to be more intellectual.

Despite the confusion that marks Nigerian daily life, I was amazed at how the people rose above it. Children could play and laugh and have fun with only a stick and an old bicycle rim. A housewife could make a dance out of pounding grain. Groups of unemployed men could spend hours discussing the problems of the world.

One phrase that I often heard in Nigeria erased all the negative impressions, at least for a minute. When people met me for the first time, although I was white, a complete stranger, and often dirty, they wouldn't say, "Hi" or "Hello." They'd say, "You are welcome," pronouncing each word clearly and with real meaning. For me, this said, "We don't have much, but what we do have is yours." And often, it was.

In eastern Nigeria, our road ended at the Cross River. We gave a cassette tape and pens to a group of boys in exchange for a ride across the river in a wooden canoe. So far we'd been on the road for almost three months, and we'd biked about 3,500 miles. Our immediate goal was to reach Ekok, Cameroon.

While in Nigeria, the team saw men from the Hausa ethnic group wear this sort of head covering.

The team bartered with local boys to be poled across the Cross River in eastern Nigeria.

PEDALING PRINCE

In eastern Nigeria, we met Dr. Opka, the head of a village clinic. When we asked him where we could pitch our tents, he pointed to a grassy patch in the clinic's courtyard and said in perfect British English, "This should serve you nicely. And then please join me for dinner."

After we'd set up our tents and changed clothes, we followed Dr. Opka to a simple restaurant where a dozen men sat around four tables. About halfway through dinner, thunder crashed and rain began to thump on the roof. An old man looked at us, raised a hand, and said something in a language we didn't understand. Dr. Opka smiled at me. "He says that you brought good fortune to our village. This is the first hard rain of the season."

"Who is that man?" I asked.

"He is a prince of our tribe," Dr. Opka answered.

Later on, as I finished my dinner, a small green lizard crawled up my leg. A man at another table shot a finger in my direction and blurted something excitedly. Again, I didn't understand.

"A further sign that you've brought good fortune to our village," replied Dr. Opka when I asked. "It's extremely rare for a lizard to come near humans."

"Who is that man?" I wanted to know.

"Another prince of our tribe."

I looked at the man who'd said that I had brought the first rain and asked, "Are you really a prince?"

He nodded his head.

I looked at the man who'd spotted the lizard on my leg and asked him the same question. He, too, was a prince. I said, "Would everyone here who is a prince please raise his hand."

Every right hand in the restaurant went up. Then the men began speaking among themselves. Dr. Opka translated for us. "For the good fortune you and your friends have brought our village, a motion has been made to crown you princes." That's how I became His Royal Excellency Dan Buettner, Prince of the Mbembe nation.

COURTING DANGER

Africa is one of the flattest continents on earth but you'd never know it cycling through Cameroon. From Ekok, just beyond the Nigerian border, the road rises from sun-baked plains into misty cool jungles where waterfalls cascade over cliffs and rickety, one-lane bridges span deep gorges. In Mamfe, still in the foothills, villagers shook their heads when we told them that we wanted to cross Cameroon's highlands.

"It's too steep," they warned. "You'll never make it on your bikes."

"Nonsense," we replied confidently. "We biked across the Sahara. The highlands can't be any worse."

They were.

Chip and Steve trudged through the steep highlands of Cameroon, at times pushing and pulling their bikes.

48

From Mamfe the road rose sharply and was built from rocks the size of bowling balls. It zigzagged up monster hills. Pedaling was impossible. Instead we pushed our 80-pound bikes, huffing and wheezing the whole way. At any point, we could look down at switchbacks we'd climbed three hours earlier.

The usual reward for pedaling uphill is the wild ride down the other side. But no such reward awaited us on the backsides of these hills. The road was so bumpy and rutted that speeds of more than five miles per hour meant wipeouts or worse. The road dropped off several hundred feet on every second switchback. To make things worse, lightning-fast flies landed on our backsides and delivered painful bites through our shorts.

Carriers of disease, tsetse flies are deadly in many parts of Africa. Tentlike traps that attract the insects help reduce the tsetse-fly population.

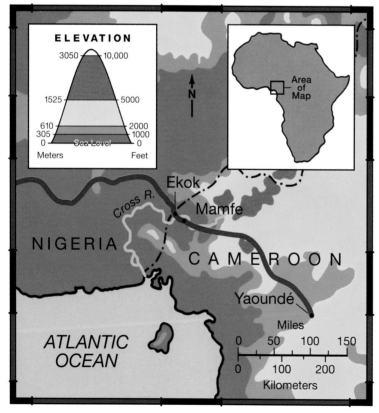

As we rode, I noticed tiny tents on top of poles outside many villages. Some of the little structures were black and purple. I asked a man walking by what they were.

"Tsetse-fly traps." he said. "We have a big problem with them. They've killed all of our cows with sleeping sickness."

I'd read about sleeping sickness. A person or an animal gets the disease by being bitten by an infected tsetse fly. Left untreated, the disease can kill.

"Why are the traps black and purple?" I asked.

"Because the tsetse fly is highly attracted to those colors."

I looked down at my bright black-and-purple bike shorts and finally understood why the flies had bothered us.

Meanwhile, I noticed that both Chip and Bo were starting to lag behind. Not long afterward, Chip came into my tent with some bad news. "Dan," he said, "I started treating Bo and myself for malaria."

"What!" I raised my voice. "How do you know that you have malaria?" Malaria, like sleeping sickness, is carried by insects and can be fatal.

"We have all of the symptoms—chills, high fever, and headache," Chip replied. "My brain feels like it's in a vise grip."

"What do you want to do?" I asked.

"We're going to take a bus to Yaoundé (the capital of Cameroon) and get tested and treated, but I'm almost sure we have it."

As Chip and Bo sped toward the capital, Steve and I jolted out of the highlands on our bikes, which were also suffering—from broken spokes, popped tires, and worn brakepads. Africa all of a sudden looked like a cruel place. We didn't want to stop and talk to people or take pictures or enjoy the lush green scenery. We just wanted to move.

Soon after reaching Cameroon, Bo *(center)*, and Chip began suffering from the first stages of malaria, a disease transmitted by mosquitoes. They bussed to Yaoundé, the capital city, for treatment.

(Above) **Rivers crisscross Cameroon, which lies just north of the equator in the west central part of Africa.**
(Left) **Dan snapped a picture of a young Cameroonian girl of the western highlands.**

We awoke at sunrise each morning, ate bread and jam, and biked until noon. After a quick lunch of chicken and rice, we napped and cycled until nightfall. Two days and 221 miles later, Steve and I rolled into Yaoundé. We were exhausted, sick with diarrhea, and my rear wheel rim was cracked beyond repair.

We found Chip and Bo camping on the tennis courts at an American-run school. They slept around the clock, waking up only to drink water and eat bananas.

As our friends recuperated, Steve and I tried to solve our bike problems. I had to replace the rear wheel rim, but there was none to be found that fit my bike. We spent an entire day looking for a spare and a second day looking for a saw to cut it to the desired measurement. It wasn't until noon on the third day that we found someone with a welder. Steve, our mechanic, did all of the work. If I had had to do the repair myself, I'd still be in Yaoundé.

Before leaving town, the four of us needed to buy visas for the next country on our trek— the Central African Republic (CAR). We went to the U.S. Embassy in Yaoundé. It had the feel of a security bank. We passed through metal detectors and were led through a locked door into a waiting room.

After 20 minutes, a bearded man called us to a service window with a bullet-proof glass. We gave him our passports through a hole.

After passing them back, he said through an intercom, "We registered your passports. Good luck with your trip. You're going to need it."

As I gathered up the passports, he added, "You know there's a civil war in Sudan."

"We're not going there," I said. "We're headed for the Central African Republic."

"That's dangerous, too."

"What would you recommend then?"

"I'm not recommending anything," he snapped. "There's no place safe in Africa. Read the embassy warnings." After delivering this grim message, he disappeared into a back office.

The U.S. **Department of State** posts warnings for countries throughout the world. The one for the Central African Republic read, "The Department of State advises U.S. citizens to defer all nonessential travel to the Central African Republic....Recent attacks by armed highway bandits in the CAR have resulted in the wounding and death of both foreigners and Central Africans...."

As soon as Dan and Steve reached Yaoundé, they set to work trying to fix Dan's wheel rim, which had cracked.

MONKEY SHINES

We spent four days in Yaoundé, repairing our bikes and waiting for Chip and Bo to get stronger. For the next week or so, we biked northeastward toward the Central African Republic. After crossing CAR's border, Chip, Steve, Bo, and I pedaled over a brown dirt road that scraped across the country's flat, grassy plains. Our goal was the town of Acocha, about 600 miles away. It was early March and sticky hot.

Houses that lined the road were constructed of mud and straw. In the afternoon, men escaped the heat by napping on mats under trees. Meanwhile, kids sat in thatched-roof schoolhouses and learned their lessons with neither books nor pen and paper. Women, like everywhere else in Africa, tended gardens, cared for children, hauled water, and cooked food.

When the sun set on the first evening, we stopped at a village called Boya. It had neither running water nor electricity, but its packed-dirt courtyards were swept clean.

While biking on a winding dirt road, the team came upon a Cameroonian school *(bottom inset)* and admired local textiles *(top inset)*.

In one such courtyard, a family—father, mother, and seven children—came together around the warmth of a cooking fire. Orange light flickered on their dark faces. I shook the man's hand, explained that we were biking across Africa, and asked if we could camp in his yard. He regarded me for several long moments. When he finally nodded to an open space next to his hut, I took it as a gesture of supreme kindness.

With flashlights in our teeth, we pitched our tents. Then a little boy invited us back to the fire where his mother was stirring two pots over the fire. One pot held boiled cassava, which looked like thick mush. We were told to wad up the cassava into little balls and dip it into the second pot.

"What's in there?" I asked pointing to the brown stew at the bottom.

"Try some," the mother answered and handed me the pot.

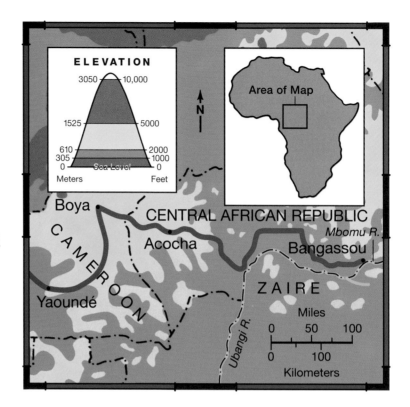

Throughout Africatrek, the team spent more than 200 nights sleeping in the courtyards of small villages.

I carved out a ball of cassava and pointed my flashlight into the pot. I saw hundreds upon hundreds of stewed centipedes in gravy! I looked around at the hungry kids eating dinner. They

Chip fed Elmer, the monkey that Dan bought in the Central African Republic.

stopped chewing their mouthfuls of dead insects and smiled at me. I gulped and handed the pot back to the mother.

"Your children are hungry, and I've already eaten," I said. "I really can't."

The next day, while I was folding up my tent, a cricket scurried out from underneath the ground cloth. One of the children snatched up the critter, singed off its wings in our campfire, and popped it into his mouth.

Six days after leaving Boya, we reached Acocha, where we unexpectedly picked up a new teammate—my own pet monkey. He weighed about three pounds and rode on the back of my bike. I named him Elmer.

I think Elmer knew he was one of the lucky monkeys in the CAR, where his kind are considered bush meat. In fact, I'd bought Elmer from a butcher who'd asked me if I wanted him cooked or raw!

Elmer traveled with me for a week. During the day, he'd chatter and laugh as I pedaled down the road. At night he'd sometimes sleep inside my shirt. Elmer did have a few bad habits, though. In the morning my sleeping bag would be littered with his little poops.

In the last town of the CAR, just before we got to the border with Zaire, I met a U.S. Peace Corps worker named Gerard who told me I'd better give up my pet.

"They'll take him away from you at the Zairian border, or they'll give you a $200 fine." (In Zaire it's illegal for foreigners to own monkeys without a permit.)

"Any ideas?" I asked.

"I'll see what I can do," Gerard said.

The next day, Gerard told me he'd talked to an African friend who'd adopt Elmer.

"How do I know he won't eat my monkey?"

"Give the man some money for Elmer's food, and he'll be in good hands."

Elmer clung to my T-shirt when I gave him away. I had to peel his little fingers off my sleeve. As I biked away, he was staring straight at me, making a sad whine. I can't say for sure, but I believe that was Elmer's way of crying.

A SOLDIER'S SURPRISE

In the Central African Republic, Steve pedaled his bike across rocks to explore a gorge.

It was mid-March 1993, when Steve, Chip, Bo, and I bicycled the last miles of the Central African Republic. We reached Bangassou, on the Mbomu River, and paid a 12-year-old boy to help us load our bikes onto his dugout canoe. No one spoke as the boy poled us slowly across the gurgling, coffee-colored waterway. On the other side lay Zaire and its thick rain forest rising out of a muddy bank.

Zaire is one of the poorest nations on the continent. The Department of State had warned us about traveling there. We'd heard about diseases—some old ones, such as malaria and leprosy, and some new ones, like Ebola.

But people who'd been to Zaire said the worst danger lay with the border guards. "They all have machine guns," claimed three British travelers we'd met. "Expect to pay bribes to get into the country."

At a clearing in the trees, our boat came to a stop with a squishy thud. We unpacked our gear and cycled a hundred yards down a dirt road before we came to a guardhouse. A young soldier stepped out.

He was wearing a baseball cap, a colorful shirt, blue jeans, and bathroom slippers. He didn't look dangerous until he pulled out a pistol and used it to wave us to the side of the road.

"Where are you coming from?" he asked in French.

"Tunisia," I replied.

"With a bicycle?"

I nodded.

"Sure!" he yelped back, not believing us.

He led us inside. The soldier sat down at a wooden table underneath a sign that read, "Taxes Collected Here" and laid his pistol on the table. Next to him, dusty cameras, Walkmans, calculators, and T-shirts filled a shelf. I figured this was "taxation" taken from the travelers who'd come before us.

Our guard began to ask questions. Yes, we really had pedaled thousands of miles from North Africa. No, no motors are in our packs.

"Don't you want to see our passports?" Steve asked after several minutes.

The soldier checked them quickly and then asked, "Do you have any money?"

Uh-oh, I thought to myself, now he's going to make us pay a bribe. I thought of the money hidden inside my handlebars and hoped he wouldn't find it.

"Just dollars," Steve said.

This soldier surprised the cyclists by giving them a wad of Zairian money to pay for bridge crossings.

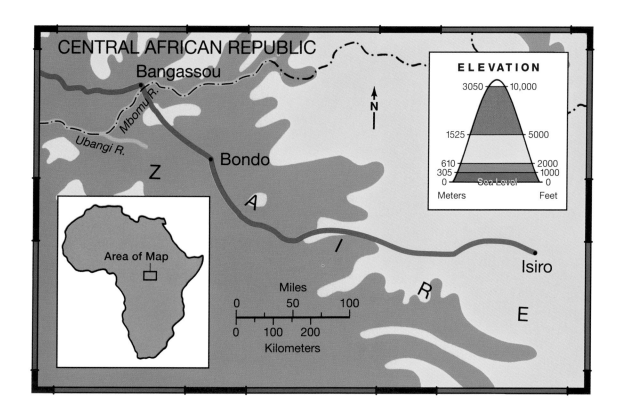

CENTRAL AFRICAN REPUBLIC

Bangassou

Mbomu R.

Ubangi R.

Z

Bondo

A

I

R

E

Isiro

N

ELEVATION

3050	10,000
1525	5000
610	2000
305	1000
0	Sea Level 0
Meters	Feet

Area of Map

Miles
0   50   100

0   100   200
Kilometers

The guard showed us a wad of Zairian money. "These are zaires. Ten dollars equals thirty million zaires." He then removed his baseball cap and counted out three hundred 100,000-zaire notes.

"There are few bridges in this region. To cross rivers, you must pay the boys who paddle the canoes. You'll need this," he said. And he *gave me* the wad of money.

"Enjoy our country," he said as a farewell.

From the border, we pedaled into the Zairian rain forest. Only thin rays of sunlight shone through the thick canopy of treetops overhead. We rode our bulky bikes over rutted paths, into potholes the size of kitchen sinks, and through thick bush. It was hard to stay on the bike without falling.

A Zairian girl carried a basket of freshly harvested fruit in the rain forest.

Sometimes there were wooden bridges *(left)* in the rain forest. Near the town of Bondo, the road was thick with mud *(below)*.

When we came to rivers and were lucky, we found bridges. But mostly there were none, and we waited for canoes to ferry us across. Twice, when no boat appeared, we hoisted our bikes on our shoulders and splashed into murky water while the beady eyes of hippopotamuses stared at us from behind snouts the size of snow shovels.

Past the city of Bondo in northeastern Zaire, the road turned muddy. We met native cyclists who pedaled battered one-speeds in worn-out thongs. They hauled huge 10-gallon jugs of cooking oil from

their Zairian villages to the Central African Republic, where they'd trade the oil for things they needed, such as needles, kerosene, pieces of fabric, and matches. Each of their six-day, 400-mile, round-trip trading journeys would earn them about $8.00.

We traveled with one of these tough merchants for three days. His name was Hervé. Our $3,000 aluminum bikes amazed him. His rickety, bent-framed bike—and how fast he could pedal it—amazed us. We could barely keep up!

Hervé really helped us. As we pedaled deeper into Zaire, the vegetation got wilder. And there were no stores or restaurants. Hervé helped us find food and spoke to the people we met along the way. He'd talk to the chief, who'd let us pitch our tents in a packed-dirt courtyard. Women would appear and lead us to a water source—usually a nearby river or spring—and we'd collect water for washing and cooking. Later Hervé would help us negotiate with the chief for dinner. We'd trade pens and dollar bills for food.

The villagers we met hunted and fished in the forest or grew cassava and peanuts in small clearings. Their only possessions were a machete, an aluminum pot, plastic dishes and spoons, and the rags they wore on their backs. To my American eyes, these people lived in misery. But as I traveled deeper into Zaire, I began to notice that the people held fast to traditional ways. Every member of the village had a feeling of belonging.

"Are these people happy?" I once asked Hervé. He gave me a puzzled look. "They have almost nothing," I said.

"These people don't know of your world," Hervé replied. "They don't know about cars and television sets and video machines so they don't miss them. What they do know is how to be satisfied with what they have. And for that, they are blessed."

Hervé, and Zairian cyclists like him, transported goods across the border into the Central African Republic, where he bartered them for supplies.

BROKEN SPIRITS, RATTLING BIKES

Four hundred and twenty-six miles of cycling in Zaire had broken our spirits and our bicycles. We were burning around 6,000 calories per day but were consuming perhaps half of that amount in food.

We mostly lived on bananas. In fact, I figured that the four of us ate an average of 145 bananas a day! We also ate cassava and, on more than one occasion, grub worms. In 18 days, our team came down with malaria, dysentery, giardiasis, and countless cases of diarrhea. We all got chiggers and intestinal worms. I lost 24 pounds.

The road had worn down to a tortured scar that ripped through the forest. It had beaten our once-proud bikes into groaning, squeaking contraptions.

Weeks of cycling in the rain forest had left the team's bikes badly battered. Here, Steve tries to repair the damage.

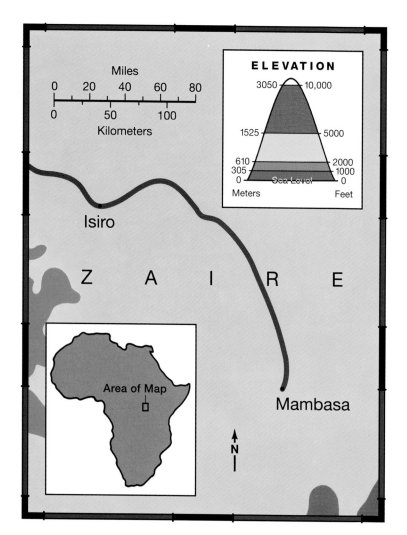

Chip, Steve, Bo, and I talked it over and decided to risk taking the shortcut. "It might be tougher," Steve said "But if it doesn't kill us it will make us stronger."

"At least we'll have some good stories to tell our grandkids," added Bo. He was only half smiling.

One of the first spots noted on the map was

OUR BODIES WERE COVERED WITH SCRAPES AND OOZING SORES.

We had all taken spills. Our bodies were covered with scrapes and oozing sores. Worse, it was late March, and the rainy season in Zaire was about to begin.

In Isiro, northeastern Zaire, the road split. On our map, we could see the better of the two routes. It arched 180 miles southward over the established "high-way" to Mambasa, Zaire. The other, more risky, route was marked with blue dots, meaning "impassable in the rainy season." The good road would take five days. The riskier option was 80 miles shorter, but we might get lost, might not find food, might run into poisonous snakes, and might meet hostile people.

the Ituri Forest, and entering it felt like going down the gullet of an enormous green beast. The road narrowed to a nearly invisible foot-path. In several places, we had to hack our way through vines and thorny branches. Every hour we got flats. I punctured my tire in five places rolling over one branch.

Encountering the Efe

We'd read about the folks who lived in the Ituri Forest. They're called the Efe. Steve and I came to a clearing and were surprised by about 20 of them. Bare-chested men wore beards and carried bows and arrows. They stood firm and stared at us. Bare-chested women sported tree-bark skirts and carried huge baskets of food they'd foraged from the forest. No one in the clan stood more than five feet tall.

"Bonjour," I said, slowing my bike to a stop and getting off. The clan members took a step back and looked at one another in bewilderment. They obviously didn't understand me.

I thrust out my hand toward the man I thought to be the leader. He looked at it for a few long seconds and then glanced at his comrades. Finally he stepped forward to shake my hand. A smile lit up his face, and the other men greeted us as well.

The Efe camp had six domed huts arranged in a semicircle around a central fire pit. Each home stood no more than four feet tall and was made of sticks and shingled with leaves. The people lived in harmony with the forest environment. Even their camp blended perfectly with the surrounding jungle.

In the Ituri Forest, Dan and Steve stopped at an Efe encampment.

Things continued to worsen. The rain, the lack of food, frequent sickness, and the bad road set up a nasty chain of events. Each day it rained longer. The holes in our path filled deeper with water and mud. We often wiped out. With more injuries came more sicknesses. Our reflexes dulled. We fell even more. It was a vicious cycle.

One day a hanging vine snagged my brake lever, launching me over the handlebars and into a mud-filled pot-hole. As I flew over the top of my bike, my calf hit the end of the handlebar. When I got up, I felt a warm trickle down the side of my leg. I could see a per-

(Above) **Steve fought to get through an overgrown section of the rain forest.** (Left) **Sometimes Dan found it easier to simply pick up his bike to move it through the vegetation.**

(Left) **The group** (from the back, Steve, Chip, Bo, and Dan) **paused at a bridge in the Zairian rain forest, perhaps the most grueling leg of Africatrek.** (Below) **Weary, sick, bandaged, and underweight, the team remained determined to get through Zaire to reach Uganda.**

fectly round, deep, bloody hole in my calf. I looked in the end of my handle bar. With my pocket knife I pried out the thick, quarter-size plug of my flesh. It made me sick.

Chip caught up with me. We had no bandages or antiseptic, so he cleansed the wound with the chlorine bleach we'd been using to purify water. It hurt like mad, but I kept pedal-

ing. With the fast-approaching rainy season—and the mud and disease that would come with it—delaying would only worsen our chances of making it across Zaire.

THE WAR ZONE

After three hard days, we reached Mambasa only to face another difficult decision, this one more serious. The final leg through Zaire to Uganda would take us on one of two pathways. The long way—via the city of Bunia—would take us five days. A much shorter route via the town of Beni would take only two. We'd heard that gunfights had broken out between the Zairian military and guerrillas from

neighboring Rwanda. Several people had been killed near the Beni road.

Again the team got together to decide. Sick, injured, and underweight, we were all desperate to get out of Zaire as quickly as possible. We had taken a risk with the last shortcut and, though difficult, we had traveled it successfully. I voted that we risk it again. Chip and Steve agreed.

"We've come this far already," interjected Bo, the voice of reason. "I don't think we should take any stupid chances."

"But we made it last time," argued Steve.

A decision to take a shortcut through a known war zone sent the cyclists into an area of thick vegetation. Bo *(inset)* felt strongly that they should play it safe by pedaling a longer route but stuck with the team when Steve, Chip, and Dan voted to take the risk.

71

Along the route, the team stopped in well-maintained villages.

We took a vote, and Bo lost. "I think this is wrong," said Bo. "But I made a commitment to this team, and I'll stay with you guys."

To our surprise, we spent a pleasant day on the best road yet. We stopped in tidy villages and occasionally found bananas or even cassava patties fried in palm oil.

Once a band of soldiers stopped us. They held machine guns and wore bandoliers of bullets. They looked at our passports and asked for bribes.

"Yes, but that was different," Bo replied. "We didn't know about the shortcut here. We know there's shooting on this road and with real guns."

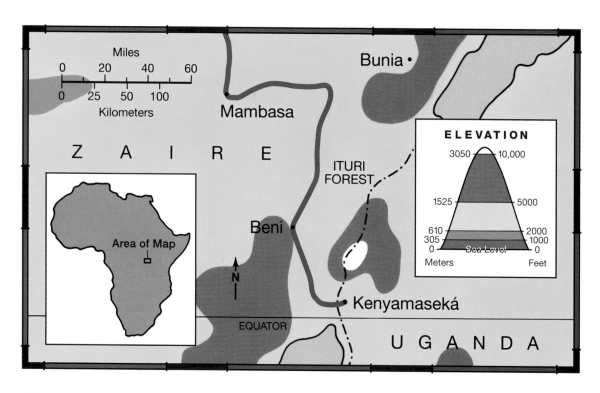

The chores of village life include pounding cassava into flour *(left)*. **Villagers often store grain in raised containers** *(below)* **to prevent insects and other animals from spoiling the food supply.**

passed through Beni soon afterward.

Toward the end of the following day—about 6,200 miles into the trek—we mounted one last hill and found ourselves on top of a steep slope overlooking Uganda's border. We'd made it! We cheered and exchanged high fives.

We sailed down the long, winding hill with the sun setting behind us. It took 30 glorious minutes to get to the bottom. Then our bubble burst.

"No!" snapped Steve. After 18 days, he was filthy dirty with wild hair and deep circles around his eyes. He glared at the soldiers. They backed off, let us pass, and *apologized* for the inconvenience. We

Heavily armed soldiers stopped the team near Beni.

At a bridge in the Zairian rain forest, heavily armed soldiers blocked the road. They wore green berets, mirrored sunglasses, and hand grenades. One of the soldiers sat behind an antiaircraft gun. Another cradled a rocket launcher. We'd clearly entered a war zone.

I squeezed my brakes to a halt. The platoon's sergeant, a muscular man of about 25, stepped forward and asked us what we were looking for in such a dangerous area.

"We're on our way to Uganda...just biking through."

"You don't want to go beyond this point," he warned.

"Why's that?" I asked.

"Guerrillas. This bridge marks the end of the government-controlled zone. Once you go across, you could be attacked. They'll steal everything you have. Maybe kill you."

"Should we go back?"

"I wouldn't do that either. It's getting dark. The guerrillas are on this side of the river, too. Just not so many of them."

That may be so, I thought, but we weren't safe staying here either. I looked around me and saw the dozen soldiers with their machine guns and bandoliers. The guy with the rocket launcher

WE'D CLEARLY ENTERED A WAR ZONE.

actually had his finger on the trigger. This bridge was obviously a military target or it wouldn't have been so heavily guarded.

I looked at my watch: 7:35 P.M. It would be dark in a few minutes. To complicate things further, Bo hadn't arrived yet. I turned to Chip. "What do you think we should do?"

"I don't know," he said. Steve shrugged.

I turned back to the sergeant. "What do you suggest?"

"I recommend that you stay here, but it's your choice. At least we have security," he replied, gesturing toward his men and their heavy weapons. This did little to put me at ease.

We set up our tents next to the soldiers' canvas barracks. They let us use their camp-fire. Although they had no pots or pans, one soldier loaned us his steel helmet to use as a pot for boiling rice.

"That's all you have to eat?" asked the sergeant. He disappeared and came back with a can of something we never dreamed we'd find in the rain forest—a can of Plum Rose Luncheon Meat. "Here," he said. "Mix this with your rice." For us the rice and the rare canned meat were a banquet.

A full moon lit the river as I stood on the bank and bathed. It was bright enough to see a flock of birds floating

Caught between two opposing armed groups, the team opted to stay in the camp of the Zairian soldiers. Bo, Steve, and Dan posed with members of the platoon before continuing on the trek.

offshore and four hippopotamuses lumbering downstream. Across the river, the moon outlined thick, fernlike vegetation. It was beautiful and scary at the same time. Were armed guerrillas lurking in those bushes? Would they attack tonight?

Later, as I lay in my sleeping bag staring up at the paper-thin ceiling of my tent, my heart raced. I believe in taking risks, but this wasn't a smart risk. We'd been warned that we were cycling into a war zone. If the bullets started flying, we wouldn't have any protection.

To make things worse, I was the leader. Although I put every decision to a vote—and three of us had voted to come here—I had the power to veto the decision. I should've done this. It wasn't only my life at stake. This stupid decision could affect the lives of my brother, my partners, and my family back home.

When I awoke the next morning, sunshine beamed through the tent. I breathed easy. We'd survived the night! We warmed up leftover rice for breakfast and broke camp. As we pedaled across the bridge

and up a long, winding hill on the other side, any kind of war seemed very far away. There was no danger after all, I said to myself. Last night was a great adventure. I felt a little silly for having worried so much.

Just then the camp we had left behind erupted in gunfire. I heard the tot-tot-tot of machine guns and then a crackling explosion. Plumes of blue smoke rose into the sky. The flock of birds that last night had been floating so serenely on the river fluttered away, squawking.

AFTER ZAIRE

Leaving Zaire felt like escaping from prison. Once across the border into Uganda, the suffocating jungle gave way to intense green fields. The road snaked through picturesque coffee, tea, and banana plantations. No longer did we hear *"Bonjour,"* from the people on the side of the road as we had in Zaire. Instead peopled greeted us with, "Good afternoon, sirs!"

We delighted as our bikes glided effortlessly

over newly paved high-ways. I pedaled up next to Bo, who'd suffered greatly while cycling through Zaire. So far for him the trip had been a chain of problems with visas, malaria, wipe-outs, and flat tires. He was bicycling with us not out of enjoyment but because he thought he could bring honor to his country.

"How do you feel?" I asked.

Bo turned to me and smiled so wide I could see his molars. "Well," he said. "I think we've entered the best part of Africa."

After leaving Zaire, the team entered Uganda, where they saw workers harvesting tea leaves by hand on large plantations.

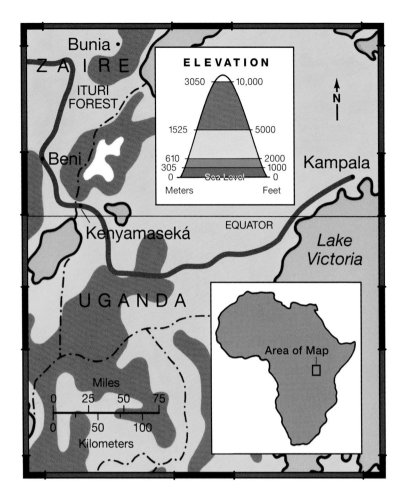

Over the next week, we pedaled over Uganda's incredibly fertile terrain. We cycled 4,000 feet into the highlands and then around Lake Victoria's northern shores. Along the way our bicycles almost completely failed us. Brakepads wore down to the metal, and stretched chains skipped over our gears. Our bodies failed us,

A banana vendor shared a paved road with a truck in Uganda.

At dusk we stopped at a small village where we found a restaurant. In a dark, dirty room lit only by a kerosene lamp we ate *chapati* (wheat pancakes), *matooke* (mashed bananas), and *nyami* (fatty meat sauce). For dessert we drank sweet spicy tea with milk in big plastic cups. After three weeks of eating in the bush, it was a feast!

too. Thirty-one days of nonstop bicycling and disease had so weakened us that we had to walk up many hills.

On April 9, 1993, when we reached Kampala, Uganda's capital, we had three things on our minds—eat, sleep, and find our new partner, Mike Mpyangu. We checked into a cheap hotel. Each day for the next week we woke at noon, ate lunch, took a nap, ate dinner, and went to bed early. Almost as if our bodies sensed that they could slack off, sicknesses surfaced. Chip's malaria flared up. Bo and I got severe diarrhea. Steve got dysentery so bad that for three days he got out of bed only to go to the bathroom and throw up.

After Steve, Bo, and I recovered, Steve took on the task of rebuilding the bikes while Bo and I went in search of Mike. (Still sick, Chip was laying low.) Bo and I walked the streets of Kampala. We talked to people at the open mar-

ket. We looked at the bus stop where vendors, beggars, travelers, buses, and vans come together in a salad of confusion. We asked about Mike at the newspaper, at the government office, and at the U.S. Embassy. Nothing.

Bicycles *(above)* were everywhere in Kampala, the capital of Uganda, and even transported meat *(below)* throughout the city.

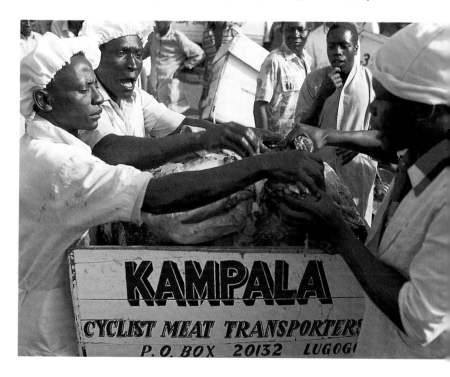

Late one afternoon, as we walked toward the hotel, a Ugandan woman recognized our Africatrek T-shirts.

"Oh my gosh," she screamed, "You must be Dan and Bo!" She threw her arms around us as Bo and I exchanged astonished glances.

She eventually told us she was Mike's friend Helen Drami. She also let us know he'd been waiting for us for a month. During that time, he'd been preparing to leave his leather business for the duration of the trek.

"We had some trouble getting through Zaire," Bo said.

"The important thing is that you're here now," exclaimed Helen. "Come on, I'll take you to Mike's house."

After a long bus ride, we came to a simple mud house with a tin roof. Mike's face lit up when he saw Bo and me. He embraced us like we were old friends.

"I thought Zaire's gorillas might have gotten you," he joked. "Come in."

Mike served us lunch of *kuku* (chicken) and *ugali* (cornmeal mash), asking us question after question. He couldn't wait to start. But during the meal I noticed that Bo had fallen silent. He sat in the chair, staring straight ahead. His

While in Kampala, Dan met up with other members of his family, including his father *(second from right)* and his brother Nick *(second from left)*. Benoît Laliberté *(far right)* also rejoined them for a while. But Kampala was also the point where Bo *(far left)* returned to Nigeria and Mike Mpyangu *(third from left)* took his place.

RECIPE FOR UGALI

Many versions of this dish exist in East Africa, and they go by different names. Zairians know the dish as *bidia,* and Malawians and Zambians call it *nsima.* In Kenya, Tanzania, and Uganda (where Dan tasted it), the doughy mixture is named *ugali.*

1 cup water   1¼ cups white cornmeal   1 cup milk

Bring a cup of water to boil in a medium saucepan. At the same time, in a bowl, gradually add ¾ cup of the cornmeal to the milk, stirring fast to make a smooth paste. Add the mixture to the boiling water, stirring constantly. Cook for 4 or 5 minutes, while adding the rest of the cornmeal. When the mixture begins to pull away from the sides of the saucepan and stick together, remove the saucepan from the heat.

Put the sticky mixture into a bowl. Then, with damp hands, shape the mixture into a ball. Turn over the ball and use the rounded sides of the bowl to help smooth the dough. Serve immediately.

East Africans traditionally tear off a small chunk of ugali and make a small groove in it with the thumb. They then use this thumb-shaped groove to scoop up sauces and stews.

closely shaved head, his wide mouth, and his glasses that he constantly pushed up with his forefinger had all become very familiar to me.

As Mike kept talking, I was thinking of the last five months that Bo and I had spent together. We'd endured one hardship after another. I suddenly felt deeply saddened. In two days, Bo would fly back to Nigeria. Just when the hardship was ending, so, too, did Bo's trip.

Soft-spoken and patient, Bo had trudged bravely through the most challenging parts of Africatrek, lending his knowledge of African languages and African customs to the team.

TALES OF EAST AFRICA

B o was right about East Africa. Paved roads, abundant food, and wonderful scenery made this leg the best part of Africatrek. From Uganda we pedaled to Kenya, down the **Great Rift Valley,** toward the capital of Nairobi. We passed extinct volcanoes, lakes teeming with pink flamingos, and big-game wildlife.

Mike turned out to be a great guide. Having operated his own business, he knew African ways of dealing with everyone—from border guards to fruit vendors. He got us the best deals. And because he spoke fluent Swahili, one of the most common languages in East Africa, he was our communication bridge to Kenya's many ethnic groups.

The landscape of East Africa made a perfect backdrop for a herd of zebras.

The team marveled at the colorful clothing and jewelry (above) of Kenya's many ethnic groups. Dan's favorite were the Masai (right), a group of whom enjoyed seeing themselves in a snapshot.

Of Kenya's roughly 70 tribal groups, the Masai were my favorite. They are a tall, handsome people who wear long, colorful robes. They have fiercely retained their independence and make their living herding cattle as they've done for centuries. Masai boys must still kill a lion to pass into manhood. The tribe's elders bargain cows and other goods to make the best marriages for Masai girls. Many of these customs seemed strange to me, but they have served these people well for a very long time.

Our team also stopped at Lake Naivasha, one of the Rift Valley's freshwater lakes and home to an incredible variety of bird species. I also learned a valuable lesson in wildlife realities. After dark, I strolled near the water and suddenly heard a sound. Something up ahead had moved. I stood still for several long minutes.

"Must've been the wind," I said to myself. Just then I heard a snort and a ground-shaking rumble. I stood dumbfounded as something charged across my path into the water.

I raced back to camp and met Steve, Mike, and an African man, a Kikuyu, who had befriended them.

"You wouldn't believe what I just saw about a hundred yards from here," I said, still breathing hard. "I scared up some huge beast. It just stampeded toward the water."

"Yeah, right," Steve laughed.

"No, really," I said. "Come on," and grabbing a flashlight, I headed toward the lake.

We scanned the water. Just a few feet offshore, we spotted two pairs of beady eyes glaring at us.

"Ooooew, very dangerous," said the Kikuyu. "It's a hippopotamus with her calf. They're the most dangerous animals in Africa."

"Most dangerous?" I said doubtingly.

"The hippo is a very angry animal. It is also very big. Sometimes they weigh 5,000 pounds. It will charge you for no reason, and if it runs into you it's like getting hit by a truck."

"Yeah, but lions and alligators can rip you to shreds," I said, still not believing that those big, innocent-looking hippos could be that dangerous.

"And you think hippos don't bite? One day a hippo came into my yard and was eating my garden. I rolled up a newspaper and tried to shoo it away. This is what happened." The man rolled up his sleeve and showed me the stub that had once been his right arm.

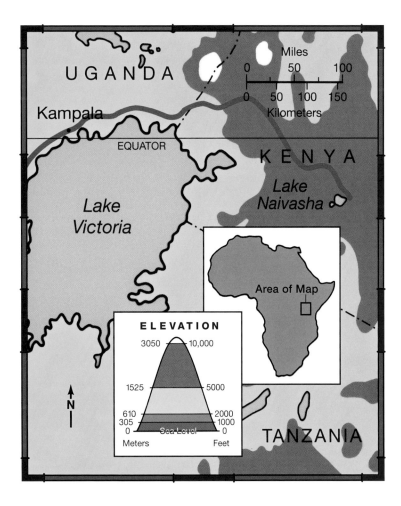

HOUSE OF GOD

In mid-May, pedaling southward across the Amboseli Plains of southern Kenya, we were still 50 miles away from Africa's tallest peak—snow-capped Mount Kiliman-jaro. The tallest freestanding mountain in the world, it towers four miles above the surrounding plains of northern Tanzania. The Masai people call it the "house of god," partly because it's so high.

For Steve and me, no African adventure would be complete without trying to scale the continent's tallest mountain. Mike and Chip had other plans. They didn't like the idea of climbing in the cold.

The team sped through the plains of Kenya to reach Tanzania, where Dan and Steve climbed Mount Kilimanjaro while Chip and Mike headed for the beaches of the island of Zanzibar.

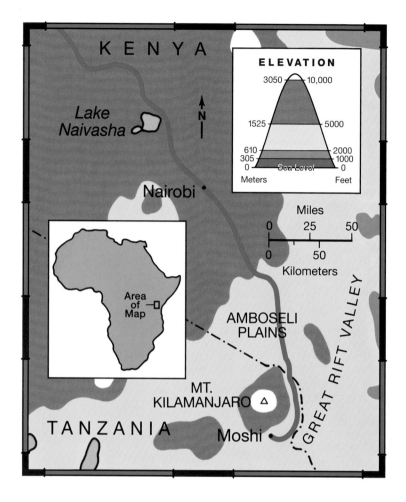

K E N Y A

Lake Naivasha

N

Nairobi

ELEVATION

3050	10,000
1525	5000
610	2000
305	1000
0	0
Meters	Feet

Sea Level

Miles
0   25   50

0   50
Kilometers

Area of Map

GREAT RIFT VALLEY

AMBOSELI PLAINS

MT. KILAMANJARO △

T A N Z A N I A   Moshi

So, when we reached the city of Moshi, at the foot of Kilimanjaro, the team split up. Mike and Chip headed for the beaches of Zanzibar (an island off Tanzania's coast), while Steve and I prepared to conquer the peak.

We'd heard much about the climb. It takes four days to make the 50-mile trek and costs up to $1,500. Although hundreds of people reach the top every year, including 75-year-old grandmothers, most people don't make it. A handful of climbers even die. Lightning strikes them or they fall. Some who climb too far too fast die from pulmonary edema, a severe sickness that happens when the lungs fill with fluid. The climbers literally drown.

Tanzanian law requires foreigners to have a guide for climbing Kilimanjaro. We chose a shy, soft-spoken teenager named Edwin who had climbed Kilimanjaro more than 20 times.

His first job was to buy food for the journey. The next day, Edwin arrived with three garbage-can-sized baskets overflowing with potatoes, carrots, tomatoes, onions, raw meat, oranges, cabbage, lard, and even a few live chickens! He also had two friends with him. "We must hire these boys to help us carry our food." Edwin also told us that we needed to rent heavy jackets. This seemed hard to believe. It was 95°F and humid.

The climb up Mount Kilimanjaro starts off easy enough. A steep but walkable trail winds through tropical rain forest, over streams, and up to Mandara Hut. We stopped there for the night. While Edwin and his friends prepared dinner, Steve and I wrote in our journals and read the logbook that people sign on the way down. "Love is like oxygen," wrote one German man. A girl from Philadelphia, Pennsylvania, summed it up in stronger terms: "This experience was one of my worst nightmares."

Day Two began in dense forest, but within an hour of climbing we broke out onto open

Edwin, Dan and Steve's guide, prepared food for them during the Kilimanjaro expedition.

savannas (grasslands) and got our first glimpse of Kilimanjaro's twin peaks. To the left, the lower but wilder Mawensi Peak loomed. To the right, the majestic dome of Kibo—our destination—disappeared in a halo of clouds.

"Pole pole," Edwin said, as he reminded us in Swahili to go slowly. The people who rush up Kilimanjaro are most likely to get altitude sickness, which happens when the body doesn't get enough oxygen from the thin air at high elevations. People suffering from altitude sickness experience shortness of breath, headaches, and dizziness.

By late afternoon, the thinner air was taking its toll. Steve and I were breathing hard just walking normally. When we reached camp at Horombo Hut, we were tired. When we woke up the next morning, the sun shone brightly. Steve and I decided to stay at this altitude and let our bodies adjust. It would improve our chances of making the summit.

Steve and I woke early for the last full day of climbing Kilimanjaro.

We reached Kibo Hut, a simple bunkhouse-like structure sitting on a barren, boulder-strewn slope in the shadow of Kilimanjaro's peak. As we pushed open the door, a Frenchman ran out with his hand over his mouth and vomited at our feet. High altitude tends to make you sick.

After a meal of boiled carrots, Steve and I crawled into our sleeping bags for a few sleepless hours of rest. Outside the wind howled. I shivered. My

head hurt. The very idea of climbing any farther seemed like a bad joke.

The final ascent to the top of Kilimanjaro—a distance of two miles straight up—began at midnight. This is because storms form on the peak shortly after sunrise, so climbers must be up and down the mountain before daybreak. My key-chain

Loaded down with food and other gear, Steve and one of the porters hired by Edwin hiked toward Horombo Hut.

At William's Point, or 16,500 feet above sea level, the thin air was beginning to weaken Dan, who later had to abandon the climb.

thermometer read –10°F. The altitude had my head feeling like there was a little man in there hammering the backs of my eyeballs. Edwin led the way. No one talked. It took every bit of energy just to put one foot in front of the other.

At about 3:30 A.M.— or 17,520 feet above sea level—we reached Hans Meyer Cave, a spot named after a German explorer who'd scaled Kilimanjaro in 1889. I sat down. A cold wind whipped down from the peak. My heart was racing, and my left side started to go numb. After a car accident a few years earlier, I had had a heart attack. I remembered a tightness in my chest and gasping for air. I was feeling the same tightness now. I just wanted to quit, go back down where humans belong. Steve shined his flashlight at me and saw the agony in my face.

THE VERY IDEA OF CLIMBING ANY FARTHER SEEMED LIKE A BAD JOKE.

"Come on," he said. "We're going down."

"Forget it," I said. "I'm not quitting."

I struggled to my feet and began walking. But it got worse. Even at a heel-to-toe pace I could only make 30 or 40 steps before I had to stop. My pounding heart kept time with my throbbing head. I stopped three times in 15 minutes. My left arm ached. I was dizzy. I felt like I was having another heart attack.

"Come on, let's go back," Steve said again. Tears came to my eyes. "No!" I snapped.

I forced myself to my feet. But my body failed me. I collapsed in a heap, shivering and dizzy. I looked up at Kibo summit. It was spinning. I had to close my eyes to make it stop. Finally I agreed to start down.

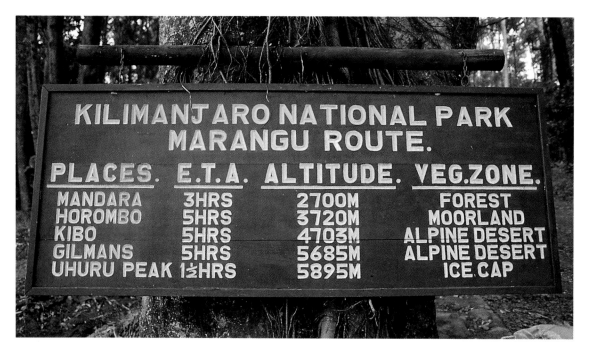

A sign shows some of the main stops on the way up Mount Kilimanjaro. The peak has two summits. Kibo, whose highest point is Uhuru Peak, is always snowcapped. Mawensi, the lower of the two summits, has no snow or ice on it.

"We're going with you," said Steve.

"No, you're not," I said. "Take my camera and get a picture at the peak."

As luck would have it, the vomiting Frenchman was on his way up with his guide. Steve joined his group, and Edwin accompanied me back down to Kibo Hut.

I followed Edwin in silence, never turning back to look at the mountain that had defeated me. I wanted to cry.

By the time we reached Kibo Hut, the violet orange of daybreak streaked the sky in the eastern horizon. I turned to Edwin.

"I'm sorry," I said.

"No problem," he replied, seeming nonetheless disappointed. Then I opened the bunkhouse door and collapsed into bed.

At noon the bunkhouse door burst open admitting the glare of the midday sun. Steve walked in breathing hard. His face was beet

red from the sun and the wind.

"Did you make it?" I asked from my sleeping bag.

"Yeah."

"To Kibo?"

"Yeah." He dropped into the bed across from me in exhaustion.

"You wouldn't have made it," he said after a minute. "It got harder. About an hour after we left you, we hit crunchy snow. We'd take three steps up and slide down two. Then we had a vertical climb to Gil-

man's Point, where we watched the sun rise. The whole time I was freezing and gasping for air. It was a nightmare."

"But how was the sunrise?" I asked.

"It was the most incredible thing I've ever seen. You could see the savannas of Kenya and the green plains of Tanzania," he said and added, "I feel as if I've seen the face of God."

We fell silent again.

"Don't worry," Steve said, sensing my disappointment. "You made the right decision. We're a team, and, like any good team, if one member succeeds, the whole team succeeds. Africatrek made it to Kilimanjaro."

Steve was right. My chest still hurt, and my arm was still numb. I dozed off realizing that my Kilimanjaro experience hadn't been a success, but it hadn't been a failure either. The only true failure is not to have tried.

Without Dan, Steve continued on and reached Gilman's Point *(top)* **and saw the sun rise on Uhuru Peak** *(above)*.

ON A ROLL

From Kilimanjaro, Steve and I bicycled southward and met Chip and Mike in Dar es Salaam, the capital of Tanzania. It was early June, and we'd pedaled almost 7,800 miles. From there, the four of us began the long, hot journey through the rest of the country.

I remember two things from this leg of the trek. In Mikumi National Park, Chip and I got off our bikes to photograph elephants. Little did we know that lurking in the bush right behind us were two Cape buffalo—among Africa's most dangerous animals. We moved quietly back to our bikes and sprinted away.

Reunited in Tanzania, the team traveled next to Malawi, whose main feature is Lake Malawi. They saw dawn break at Cape McLear *(right)*, on the lake's southern shore.

The other thing I remember was that there was almost no fresh water. In several villages, we had to buy water from kids who brought it up from nearby rivers in big cans.

This route eventually took us to Malawi, a long, skinny neighbor to Tanzania. Most Malawians make their living as farmers or plantation

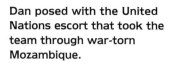

Dan posed with the United Nations escort that took the team through war-torn Mozambique.

Villagers haul in small fish from the waters of Lake Malawi.

workers. The country holds wildlife parks where the animals are well protected. It also has spectacular mountains and, of course, the country's jewel, Lake Malawi.

Most of our 400-mile ride through Malawi traced the lake's shore. At night we'd camp in fishing villages where people ate the same cornmeal mash that Africans from Uganda to South Africa eat. The one notable addition to the menu was fish. Sometimes we'd find delicious roasted fish called *chambo.* Other villages, however, served what looked like dried minnows—the type available in American bait shops.

At Cape McLear, along Lake Malawi's southern shore, Steve came down with malaria. We set up camp on the beach and waited three days for him to recuperate. Steve's bad luck was our good fortune. Cape McLear was a tropical paradise where the people of a traditional African village welcome travelers. While my brother stayed in the tent shivering with fever, Mike, Chip, and I spent our days snorkeling in the lake. The crystal clear water and colorful fish made us

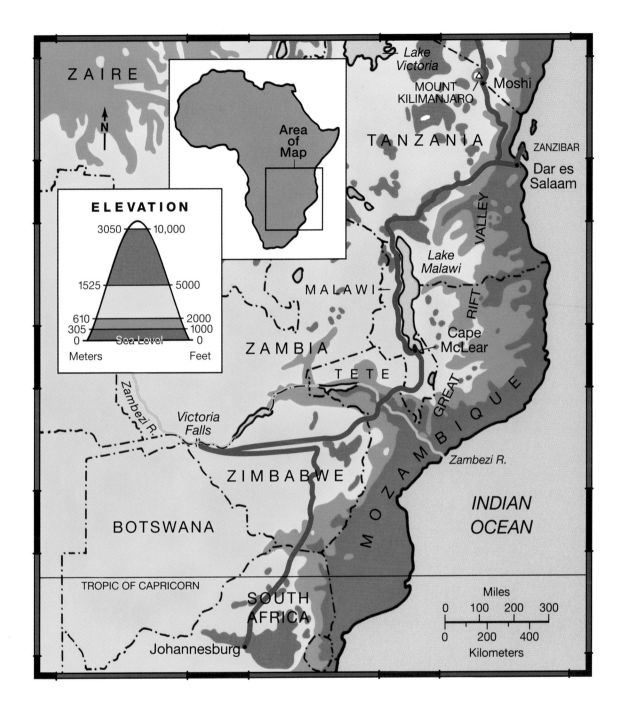

feel like we were swimming in a huge aquarium.

Things took a turn for the worse as we biked across the border into Mozambique, where years of civil war had torn up the countryside. Our route led us down the Tete Corridor, a 180-mile stretch of road also known as Machine Gun Alley. As we cycled down the corridor, heavily armed United Nations soldiers escorted us. We didn't waste time and were out of Mozambique in three days.

After we crossed the Mozambican border, this time into Zimbabwe, we noticed that people wore shoes—a sign of wealth—and that the road was nicely paved. Unlike in Mozambique, we could wander into nearby fields for a picnic without worrying about stepping on a land mine. Then we took a detour to Victoria Falls.

The local name for the falls is Mosiatunya or "the smoke that thunders." Every minute millions of gallons of water from the Zambezi River crash like thunder into a 330-foot gorge. Clouds of smokelike spray shoot 1,500 feet into the air. On a sunny day, the most brilliant rainbow imaginable arches out of the chasm. Just days after

the squalor of Mozambique, we found ourselves at one of the most spectacular and memorable spots in the world.

Perhaps we saw the biggest contrast in Johannesburg, South Africa. In many ways, Africa had been what I expected. We saw rain forests in Zaire, wild animals in Kenya, and colorfully dressed peoples everywhere. In late July, in Johannesburg, I was greeted by the sight of 30-story high-rises, computerized offices hooked to the Internet, and Pizza Hut restaurants.

The Africatrek team was a big deal for a few days in South Africa. We appeared on television, in the newspaper, and on radio. Walter Sisulu, the vice chairperson of the African National Congress (ANC)—a mostly black organization working for change in South Africa—invited us to his office. Soon thereafter, then-president F. W. de Klerk invited us to the

Victoria Falls, on Zimbabwe's border with Zambia, is more than a mile wide and sends a huge volume of water from the Zambezi River crashing into a deep gorge.

In South Africa, the team witnessed the first election campaign in which all South Africans could vote. This youth holds posters of Chris Hani, a leader of the African National Congress, who had recently been killed.

The then-president of South Africa, F. W. de Klerk, invited the team to visit with him at the presidential palace in Pretoria.

impossible feat. This was an important message in South Africa. White people are a minority in the country but had controlled its businesses and government for hundreds of years.

When we arrived, Nelson Mandela, the ANC's leader, had recently been freed from prison and was running for president. For the first time, all adults—black and white—would be able to vote. Most South Africans were sure that Mandela would win the election. But would the transition succeed or would a war erupt between black South Africans and white South Africans? No one knew for sure. One thing was clear. The future of the nation depended on cooperation between all parts of its diverse population.

presidential palace, a building that looks like a seventeenth-century European castle.

We were honored not just because we had biked across Africa but because we had done so as a multiethnic, multinational team. We had cooperated and accomplished a seemingly

THE END
OF THE ROAD

The last thousand or so miles of Africatrek went quickly. From Johannesburg we cycled southward through Bethlehem, Ficksburg, and the Golden Gate (South Africa's Grand Canyon).

At Port Elizabeth on the Indian Ocean, we turned westward along the Garden Route—the popular name for the Port-Elizabeth-to-Capetown highway that traces South Africa's southernmost coast. To our left, we caught regular glimpses of the ocean's cobalt blue waters. To the right, flower-studded hills rolled away from the road. We crossed yawning gorges, cycled down winding forest roads, and even stayed in a hip surfing village called J-Bay (Jeffreys Bay). People there wore neon green and used words like "dude" and "gnarly."

As Africatrek neared its destination, Dan raised his bike in jubilation at the Golden Gate in central South Africa.

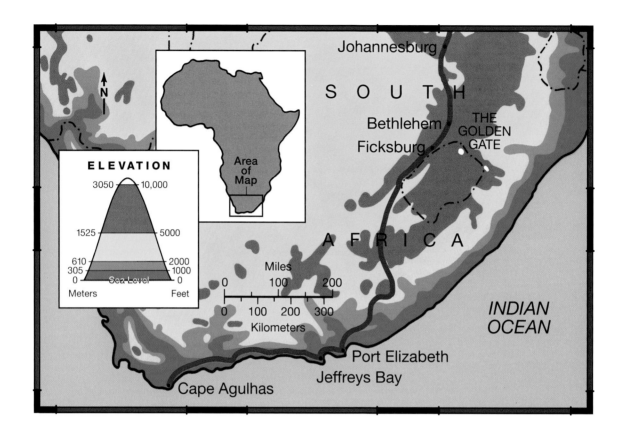

On August 17, 1993, Steve, Chip, Mike, and I coasted through the sleepy village of Cape Agulhas at the continent's southernmost tip. Cozy cottages and a red-and-white lighthouse were surrounded by fields of heather. A gray mist hung over both land and sea.

At 4:17 P.M., we pushed our bikes over the pebbly beach and rolled our front wheels into the ocean. We thus ended a 262-day journey that had begun with

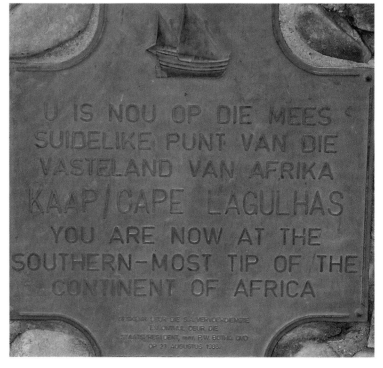

The sign at Cape Agulhas confirmed that the team had reached their goal.

our rear wheels in the Mediterranean Sea.

Eleven thousand, eight hundred, and fifty-five cycling miles and millions of pedal turns after leaving Bizerte, Tunisia, our journey ended. We exchanged high fives and felt the thrill of setting a Guinness Book world record. Then a strange silence fell over us.

We stood at Cape Agulhas looking at the cold, choppy sea and the dingy sky. Chip would soon return to his Navajo clinic in Arizona. Mike would go back to his leather factory in Kampala. Steve and I would return to Minnesota and dream up another expedition. The hardships of bicycling Africa were over, but so too were the adventures.

Steve, Dan, Mike, and Chip struck a formal pose at the southernmost tip of the African continent.

EPILOGUE

We had crossed 14 African countries at a time when the continent was changing rapidly. We'd noticed that traditional customs and ways of making a living were being replaced with modern methods. Africa's population is growing faster than that of any other continent. Local economies have to go full speed ahead just to stand still.

We also saw reasons for hope. In more than half the countries on

our route, elected presidents had recently replaced corrupt dictators, bringing the promise of better leadership. Africa continues to have great economic potential, with huge diamond mines, extensive gold deposits, and fertile farmland. And the children of Africa, more so than ever, are getting an education.

I got an education, too. I learned about Africa's people, geography, and customs firsthand as I slowly pedaled the continent's vastness. Having lived with Chip, Mike, and Bo, I got an unforgettable lesson about the difficulties that confront black people. I learned about myself. If I could survive in Africa, I could face any challenge back home.

Despite a slower pace, my life would never be the same. Africatrek had permanently marked my soul.

I was leaving Africa, but I knew Africa would never completely leave me.

AUTHOR'S ACKNOWLEDGMENTS

Generous sponsors are a big part of successful expeditions like Africatrek. Chip, Steve, Bo, Mike, and I would like to thank Target Stores (especially Bob Thacker), 3M Scotchlite, and WTC/Ecomaster for making our expedition possible. Cannondale bicycles, which carried us across Africa, served us like dependable friends. PentaPure Oasis purifiers kept us disease free even when drinking the dirtiest water. The Trimble GPS helped us find our way. Blackburn Racks and the mighty Overland Packs carried our gear. Freewheel Bicycles kept us rolling.

Of the hundreds of individuals who helped us, we'd especially like to thank Janine Thull, Dan Eckberg, Tony Kantar, Gerry Richman, John Ricter, Roger Hale, Chris Hedlund, Rafaela Salido, Pat McKeon, Roger and Dolly Buettner, Angelo and Irene Palermo, and Nick Buettner.

Of the countless Africans who opened their hearts and homes to us, one kind soul stands out—Helen Drami, Mike's friend in Uganda. We never had a chance to properly thank her for her hospitality. Nor will we ever. She died of tuberculosis in 1993.

Nystrom Division of Herff-Jones printed the study guide—written by Hamline University's Center for Global Environmental Education—that we gave to 52,000 schools. National Camera Exchange helped us with the cameras. Howard Hanson at Pro-

Color provided the film and developing necessary to shoot the pictures in this book. Kjell Bergh and his Borton Travel made all our complex travel arrangements. Finally the amazing Jocey Hale held everything together at Africatrek headquarters.

Recognition must also go to Dave Porter, Don Kuplic, and Rotary International who undertook the massive task of collecting, repairing, and shipping 1,004 bicycles to East Africa in collaboration with Africatrek.

We'd like to thank MECC/SoftKey for creating *Africa Trail,* the interactive CD-ROM, Janice McDonald for producing our 12 CNN segments, Emily Goldberg and KTCA television for producing the Emmy award–winning documentary on Africatrek, and Lerner Publications Company for publishing this book. Through their efforts, our expedition will live on for a long time to come.

USED BY THE AFRICATREK TEAM

12 55-gallon drums of soda pop

35 yards of dental floss

96 antimalaria tablets

500 painkillers

80 diarrhea tablets

327 flat tire patches

32 spare tires

120 AA batteries

80 rolls of toilet paper

238 rolls of film

PRONUNCIATION GUIDE

Bangassou	bahn-GAH-soo
Benoît Laliberté	BUHN-wah lah-lih-behr-TAY
Bizerte	buh-ZERT-ee
Dar es Salaam	dahr ehs'suh-LAHM
Djelfa	JEHL-fuh
djellaba	juh-LAH-buh
Djerma	JERM-ah
Efe	AY-fay
Ghardaïa	gahr-DAH-yuh
Hervé	ehr-VAY
In Guezzam	ihn geh-ZAHM
In Salah	ihn suh-LAH
Kikuyu	kee-KOO-yoo
Kilimanjaro	kihl-uh-muhn-JAHR-oh
Laghouat	lah-GWAHT
Maghrib	mah-GREEB
Masai	mah-SYE
Mbomu	mm-BOH-moo
Mbembe	mm-BEHM-bee
Mobolaji Oduyoye	moh-boh-LAH-jee oh-doh-YOH-yeh
Mpyangu	mm-PYAHN-goo
Mzabite	mm-zah-BEE-tee
Niger	NY-juhr
Swahili	swah-HEE-lee
Tanezrouft	tah-nehz-ROOFT
tsetse	TZEHT-see
Tuareg	TWAH-rehg
Uganda	yoo-GAHN-duh
Yaoundé	yah-OON-day
ugali	oo-GAH-lee

South Africans decorated this doorway with colorful geometric designs.

GLOSSARY

Department of State: An organization within the U.S. government that, among its other duties, protects U.S. citizens who are traveling abroad.

dreadlocks: A hairstyle made up of narrow, ropelike strands of hair formed by matting or braiding.

East Africa: An unofficial region of the African continent that usually includes the nations of Kenya, Tanzania, Uganda, Rwanda, Burundi, and Malawi.

erg: A shifting sand dune in the Sahara Desert. Some ergs can be quite large, such as those in Algeria and Mali.

Great Rift Valley: A long, steep, narrow valley that stretches from the Middle East to East Africa. The rift formed when land sank between two roughly parallel faults (cracks in the earth). Along the rift are seas, gulfs, and lakes, including Lake Malawi and Lake Naivasha.

harmattan: A strong wind that happens in West Africa. Harmattans, which blow directly off the Sahara Desert, are usually hot, dry, and dusty. They can form a thick haze that hampers travel and navigation and that can harm crops.

Islam: A one-God religion founded on the Arabian Peninsula in the seventh century A.D. Muslims (followers of Islam) brought the faith to North Africa soon afterward, and it eventually spread to all corners of the continent.

Maghrib: An Arabic term meaning "the west" that Arabic-speaking Muslims gave to lands northwest of the Arabian Peninsula in the seventh century A.D.

A sand dune provided a place to rest one of the trek's mountain bikes.

While in a village, Chip stopped to make a nourishing drink.

North Africa: An unofficial region of the African continent that usually includes Morocco, Algeria, Tunisia, Libya, and Egypt.

oasis: A fertile area of a desert that is usually fed by an underground source of water. Oases vary in size from a small patch surrounded by date palms to a large city that raises yearly crops.

Sahel: An Arabic word meaning "coast" that refers to the belt of land bordering the southern edge of the Sahara Desert.

savanna: A tropical grassland where annual rainfall varies from season to season.

sirocco: The southerly wind that happens in North Africa and southern Italy. Arriving from the Sahara, the sirocco is hot, dry, and often full of dust.

southern Africa: An unofficial region of the African continent that is not to be confused with the nation of South Africa. Among southern African countries are Namibia, Botswana, Zimbabwe, Mozambique, South Africa, and Lesotho.

sub-Saharan Africa: The area of the African continent that lies south of the Sahara Desert.

Tanezrouft: A section of the Sahara Desert in southern Algeria.

trans-Saharan Highway: A 900-mile paved road that spans part of the Sahara Desert from Algiers, Algeria, to Tamanrasset, Algeria.

wadi: A usually dry desert waterway that holds water only after a heavy rainfall.

West Africa: An unofficial region of the African continent that includes coastal and semidesert landlocked countries. Among the nations of West Africa are Senegal, Ghana, Mali, Niger, and Nigeria.

INDEX

METRIC CONVERSION CHART		
WHEN YOU KNOW:	MULTIPLY BY:	TO FIND:
cups (liquid measure)	.237	liters
cups (dry measure)	.275	liters
pounds	.454	kilograms
gallons	3.78	liters
feet	.3048	meters
yards	.9144	meters
miles	1.609	kilometers
degrees Fahrenheit	5/9 (after subtracting 32)	degrees Celsius